COWTOONS

Living with Cows

BOB ARTLEY's

COWTOONS

Living with Cows

By Bob Artley

Voyageur Press

From the Newspaper Series "Memories of a Former Kid"

Printed in China

04   05   06   07   08   5   4   3   2   1

Library of Congress Cataloging-in-Publication Data available

ISBN 0-89658-614-6

Distributed in Canada by Raincoast Books
9050 Shaughnessy Street, Vancouver, B.C. V6P 6E5

Published by Voyageur Press, Inc.
123 North Second Street, P.O. Box 338, Stillwater, MN 55082 U.S.A.
651-430-2210, fax 651-430-2211
books@voyageurpress.com
www.voyageurpress.com

For my wife, Margaret,

a constant help and inspiration in my work, and one

who, at an early age, became acquainted with cows

Contents

Acknowledgment

The material in this book is selected from the syndicated cartoon series, "Memories of a Former Kid," distributed by Extra Newspaper Features of Rochester, Minnesota, and Mug Wump Marketing of Hampton, Iowa, and appearing in publications throughout the country. In order to have a complete collection of Artley cartoons dealing with cows, this volume includes several drawings that have appeared in previous Bob Artley books: *Memories of a Former Kid, Cartoons,* and *Cartoons II.*

PREFACE

Just how far back in the mists of time the cow became an integral part of the human experience, I do not know. But I do know that my own experience with that wonderful creature began way back in *my* dim and distant past. For as long as I can remember cows and I were involved in a love-hate relationship that has had a lasting effect on me. One might say that I bonded with cows at an early age.

The contents of this book represent the entire gamut of emotions experienced by my brothers and me through our close association with the bovine herd on our farm during the 1920s and 30s. And, speaking for myself, cows are high on my list of our fellow creatures on this planet for which I feel genuine affection.

To this day, the warm friendly smell of a cow barn or cattle shed evokes in me nostalgia for a time and place where cows were very much a part of my growing-up years on our family farm.

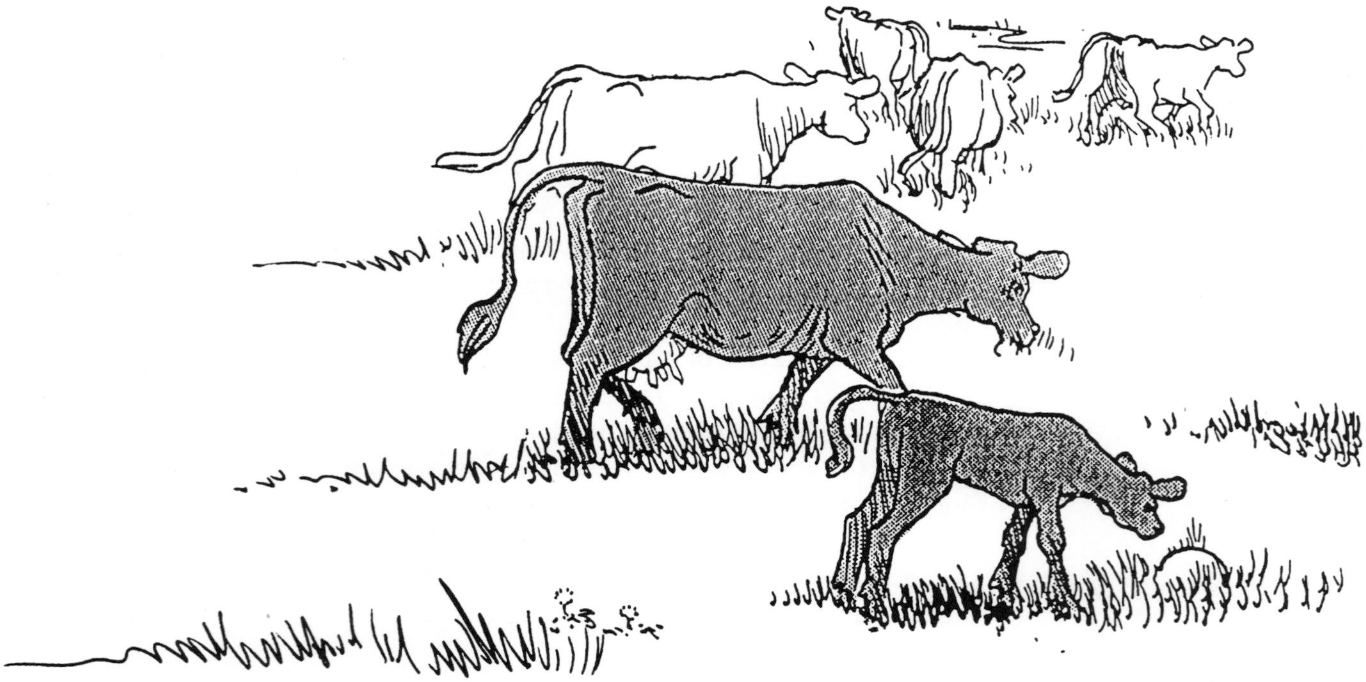

BOB ARTLEY's COWTOONS

Mud

When Iowa Highway 10 (now 3), which crosses the state east and west about a mile south of our farm, was upgraded from gravel to concrete in the 1920s, Dad made the wistful comment that it would be nice to have just a small portion of all that paved surface in our cow yard.

This impossible dream was one that we all shared during the belly-deep mud days of the early spring thaws and the rainy seasons of spring and fall.

A spring-fed creek meandered through our pasture, making sloughs and mud holes that the cows frequented. They would seek out these soggy places in an attempt to escape the torment of biting flies that gathered on their legs and bellies. So when we brought the cows in for milking, it was necessary to clean their udders and the surrounding area in an effort to keep the milk clean.

The sloppy mixture of mud and manure in the cow yard in early spring caused us to think longingly of the frigid winter weather when the surface was frozen solid and the cows kept comparatively clean. Thus our joy in the first balmy days of spring was somewhat tempered by the prospect of muddy days that lay ahead.

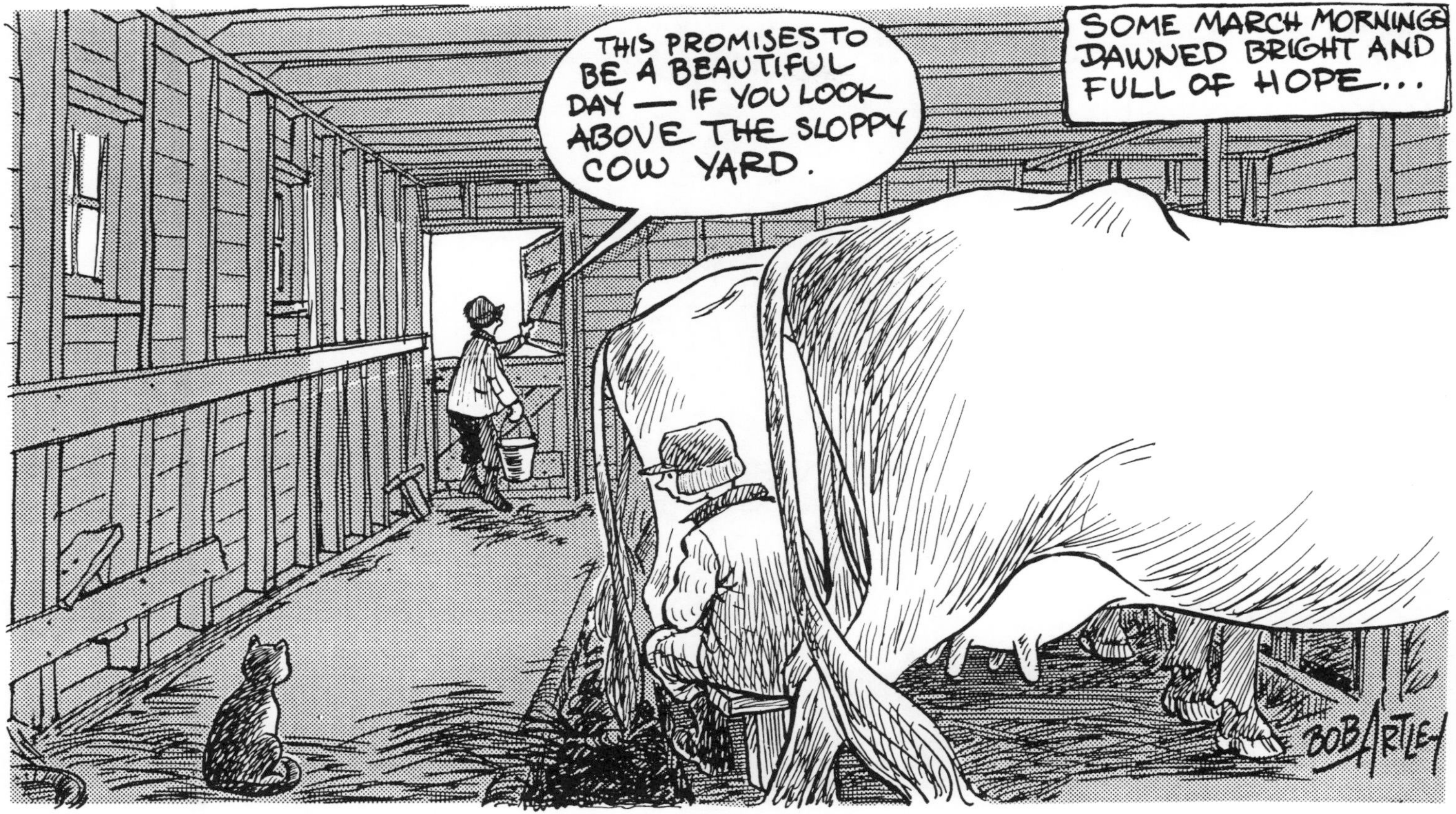
SOME MARCH MORNINGS DAWNED BRIGHT AND FULL OF HOPE...
THIS PROMISES TO BE A BEAUTIFUL DAY — IF YOU LOOK ABOVE THE SLOPPY COW YARD.
BOB ARTLEY

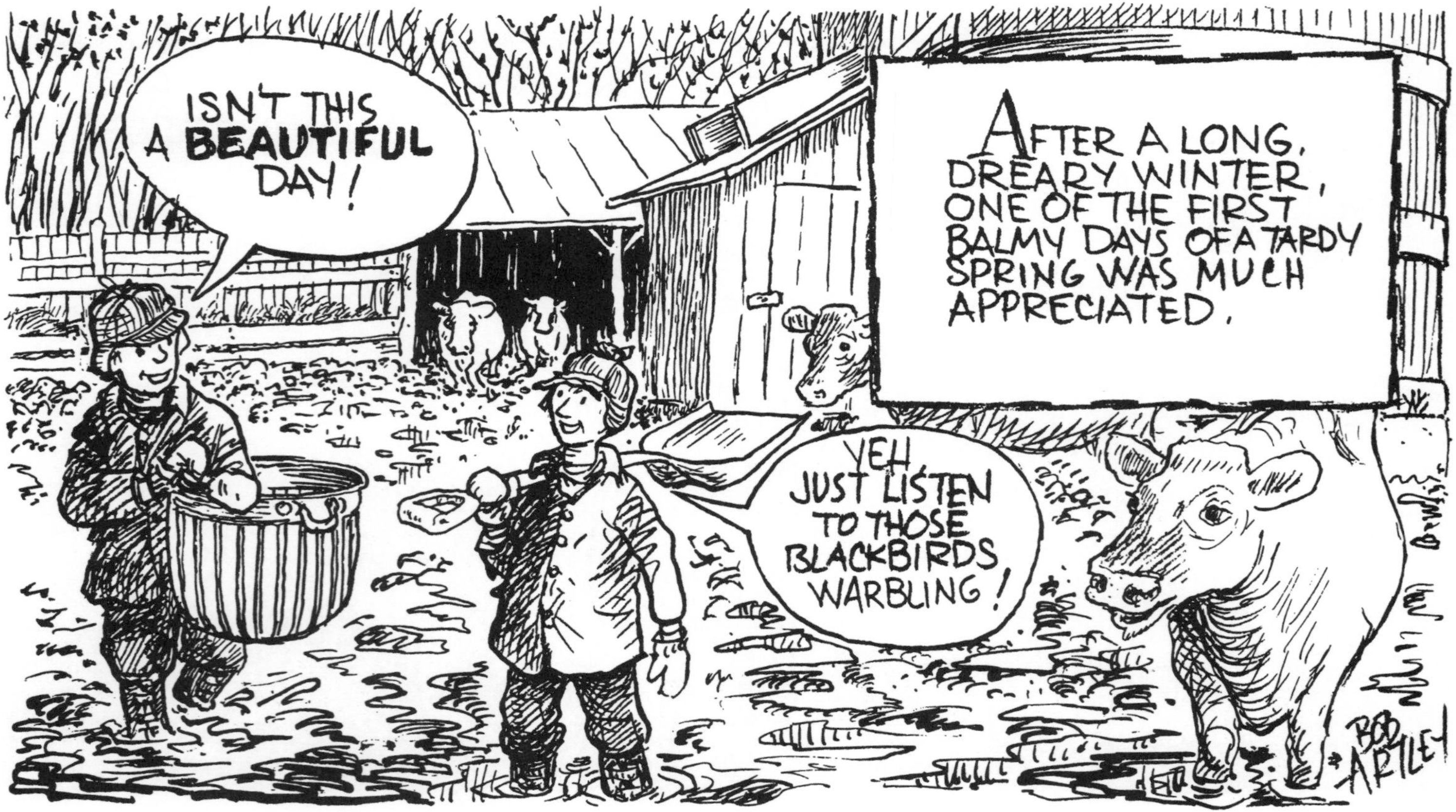
ISN'T THIS A **BEAUTIFUL** DAY!
AFTER A LONG, DREARY WINTER, ONE OF THE FIRST BALMY DAYS OF A TARDY SPRING WAS MUCH APPRECIATED.
YEH, JUST LISTEN TO THOSE BLACKBIRDS WARBLING!
BOB ARTLEY

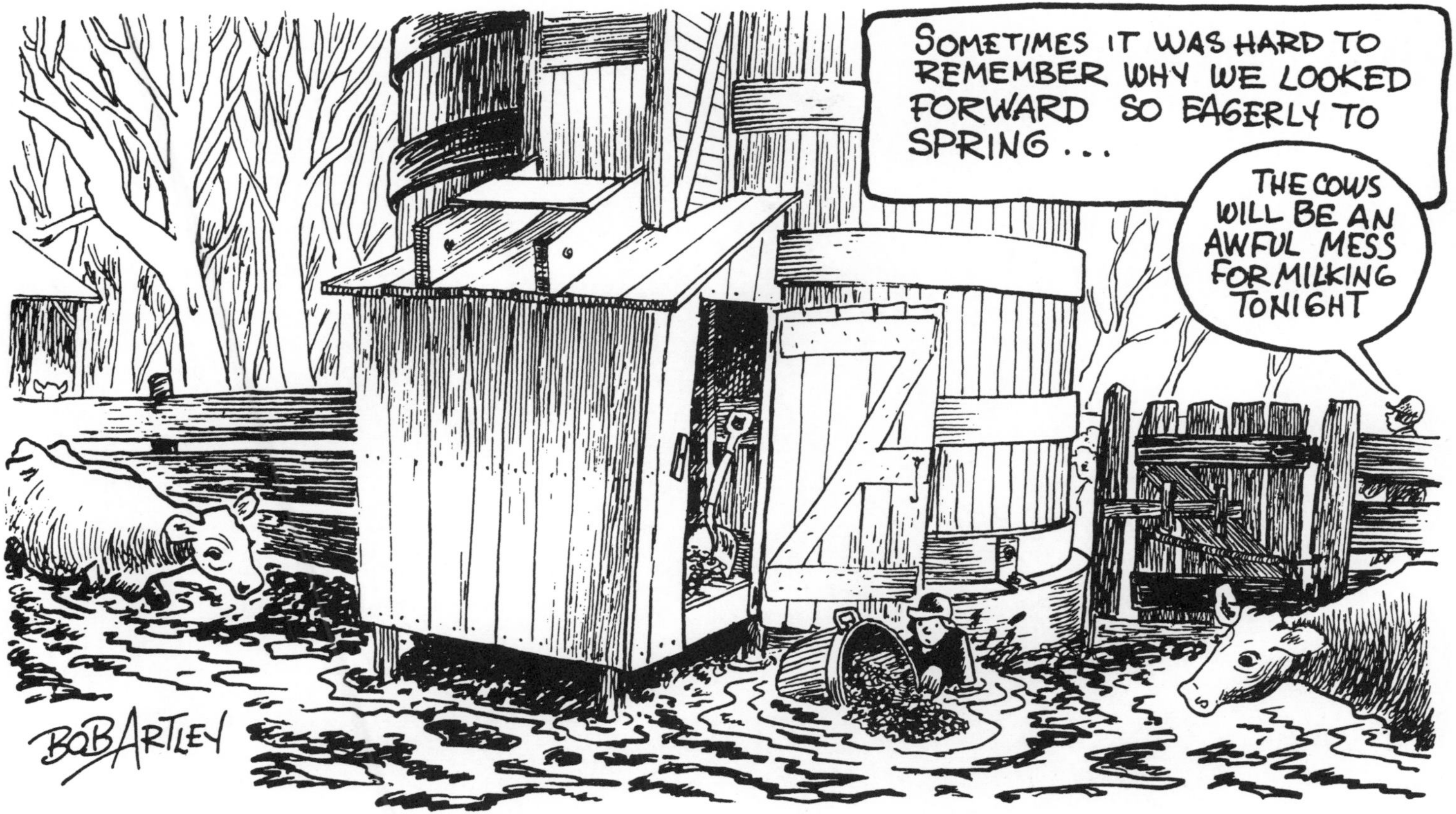
SOMETIMES IT WAS HARD TO REMEMBER WHY WE LOOKED FORWARD SO EAGERLY TO SPRING . . .
THE COWS WILL BE AN AWFUL MESS FOR MILKING TONIGHT
BOB ARTLEY

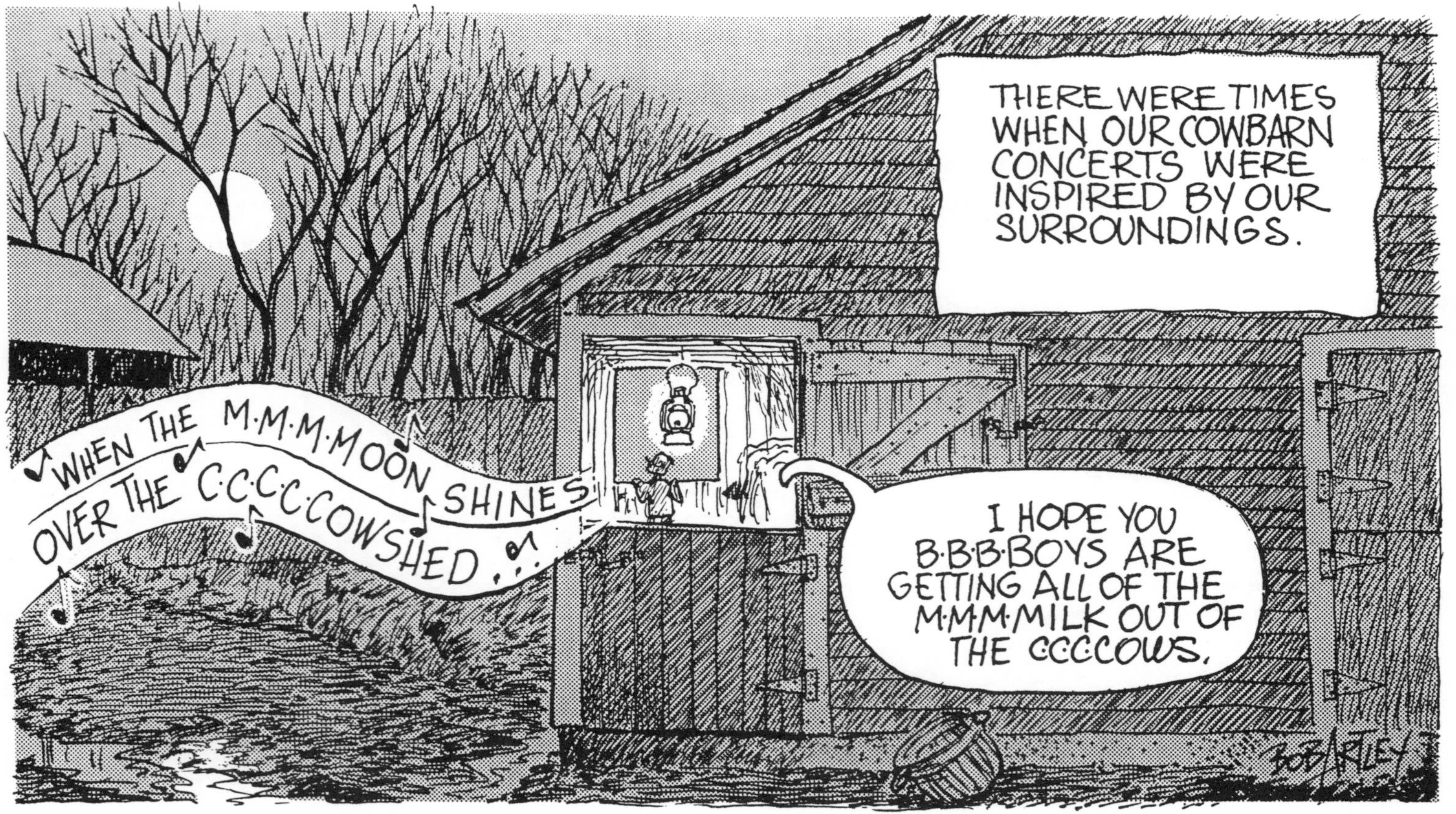
THERE WERE TIMES WHEN OUR COWBARN CONCERTS WERE INSPIRED BY OUR SURROUNDINGS.
WHEN THE M·M·M·MOON SHINES OVER THE C·C·C·C·C·COWSHED.
I HOPE YOU B·B·B·BOYS ARE GETTING ALL OF THE M·M·M·MILK OUT OF THE C·C·C·COWS.
BOB ARTLEY

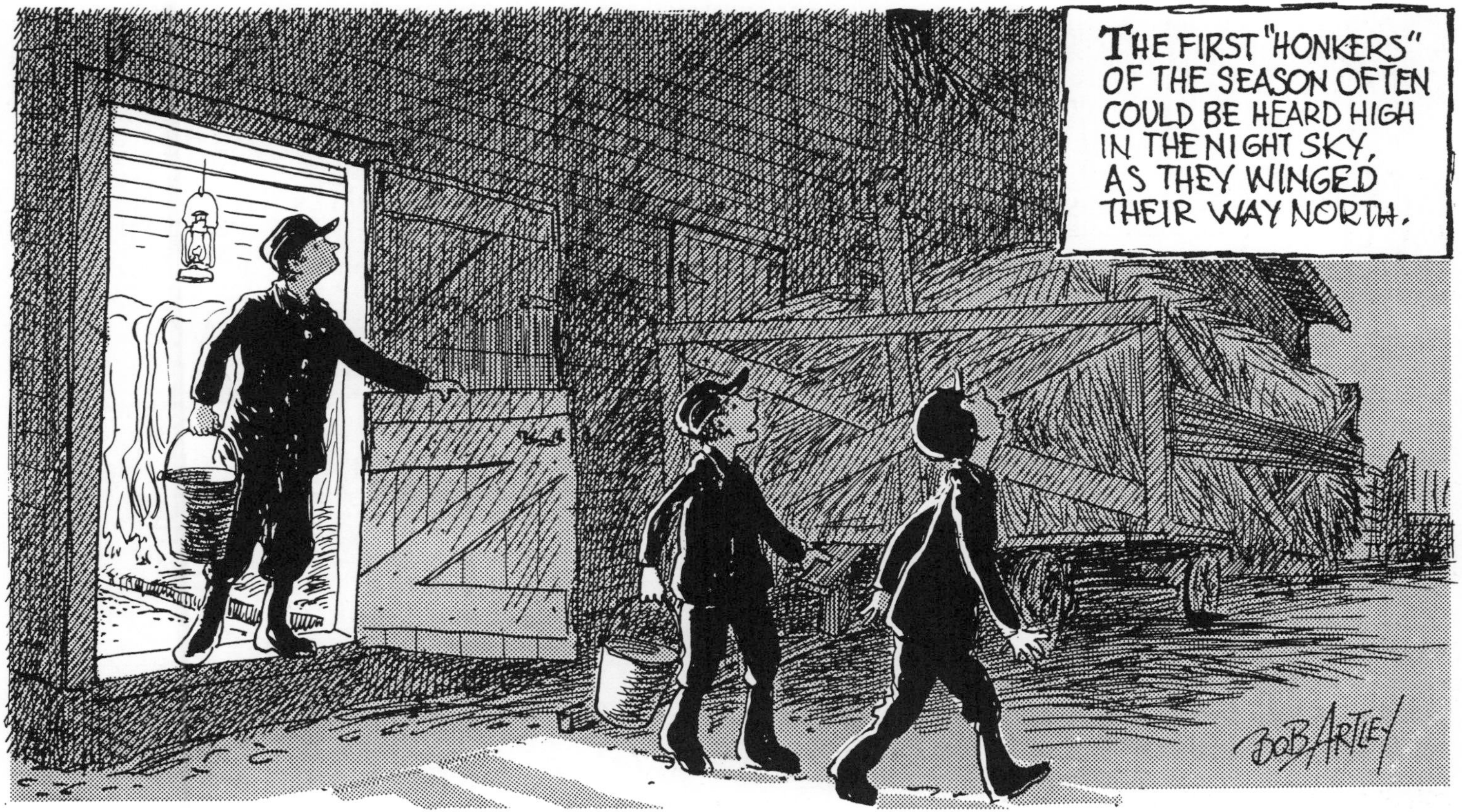
THE FIRST "HONKERS" OF THE SEASON OFTEN COULD BE HEARD HIGH IN THE NIGHT SKY, AS THEY WINGED THEIR WAY NORTH.
BOB ARTLEY

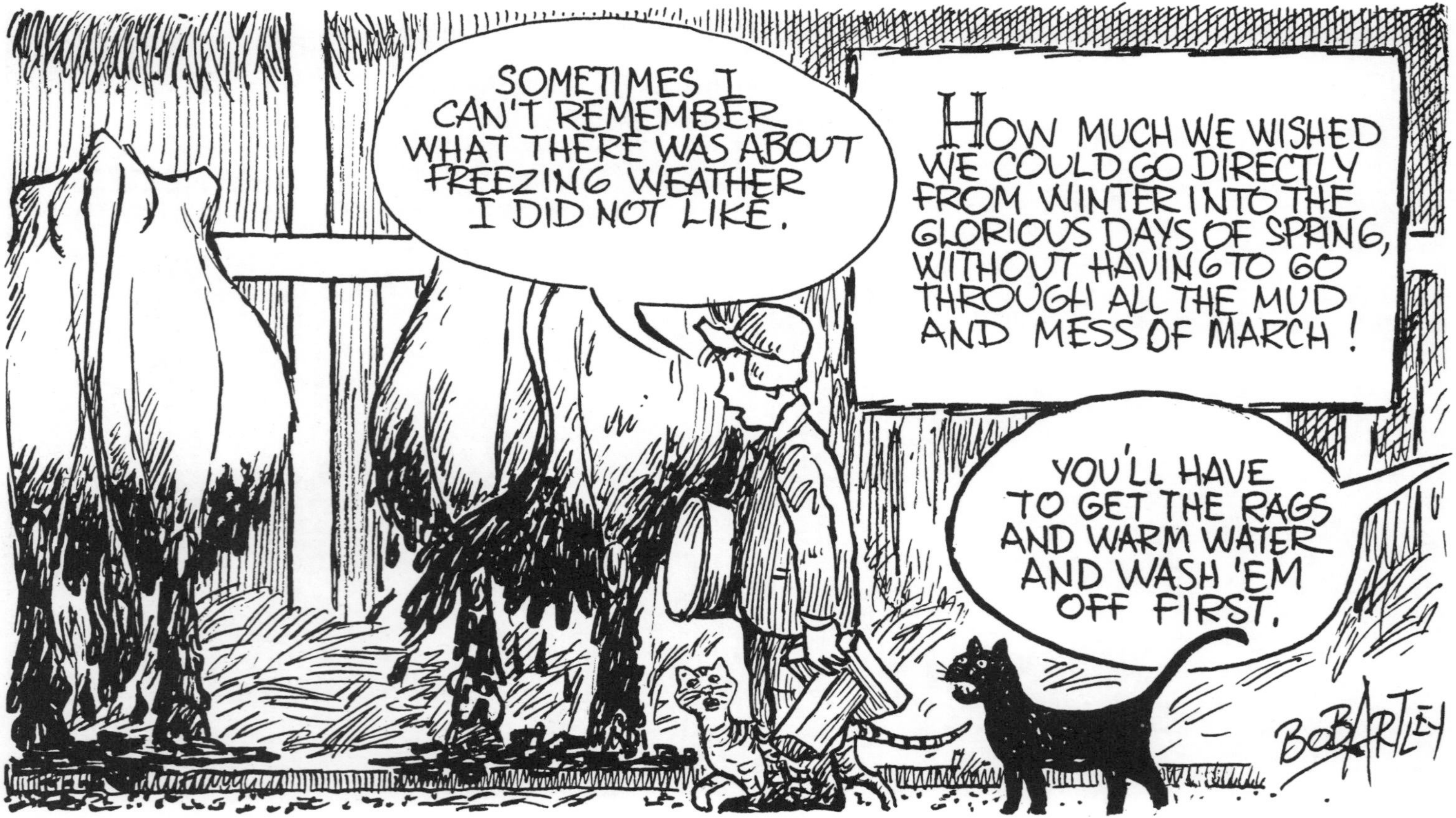
SOMETIMES I CAN'T REMEMBER WHAT THERE WAS ABOUT FREEZING WEATHER I DID NOT LIKE.
HOW MUCH WE WISHED WE COULD GO DIRECTLY FROM WINTER INTO THE GLORIOUS DAYS OF SPRING, WITHOUT HAVING TO GO THROUGH ALL THE MUD AND MESS OF MARCH!
YOU'LL HAVE TO GET THE RAGS AND WARM WATER AND WASH 'EM OFF FIRST.
BOBARTLEY

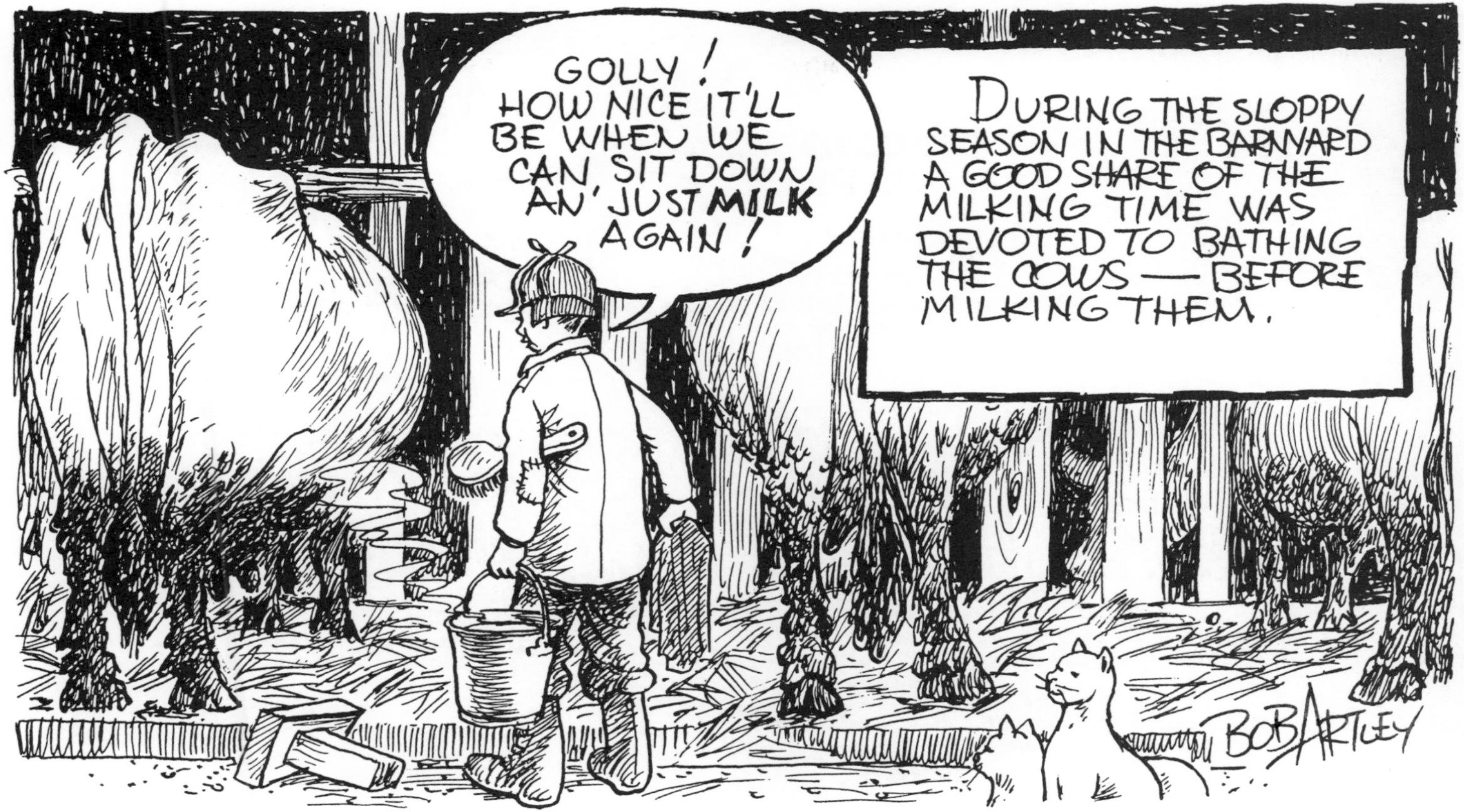
GOLLY! HOW NICE IT'LL BE WHEN WE CAN, SIT DOWN AN' JUST MILK AGAIN!
DURING THE SLOPPY SEASON IN THE BARNYARD A GOOD SHARE OF THE MILKING TIME WAS DEVOTED TO BATHING THE COWS — BEFORE MILKING THEM.
BOB ARTLEY

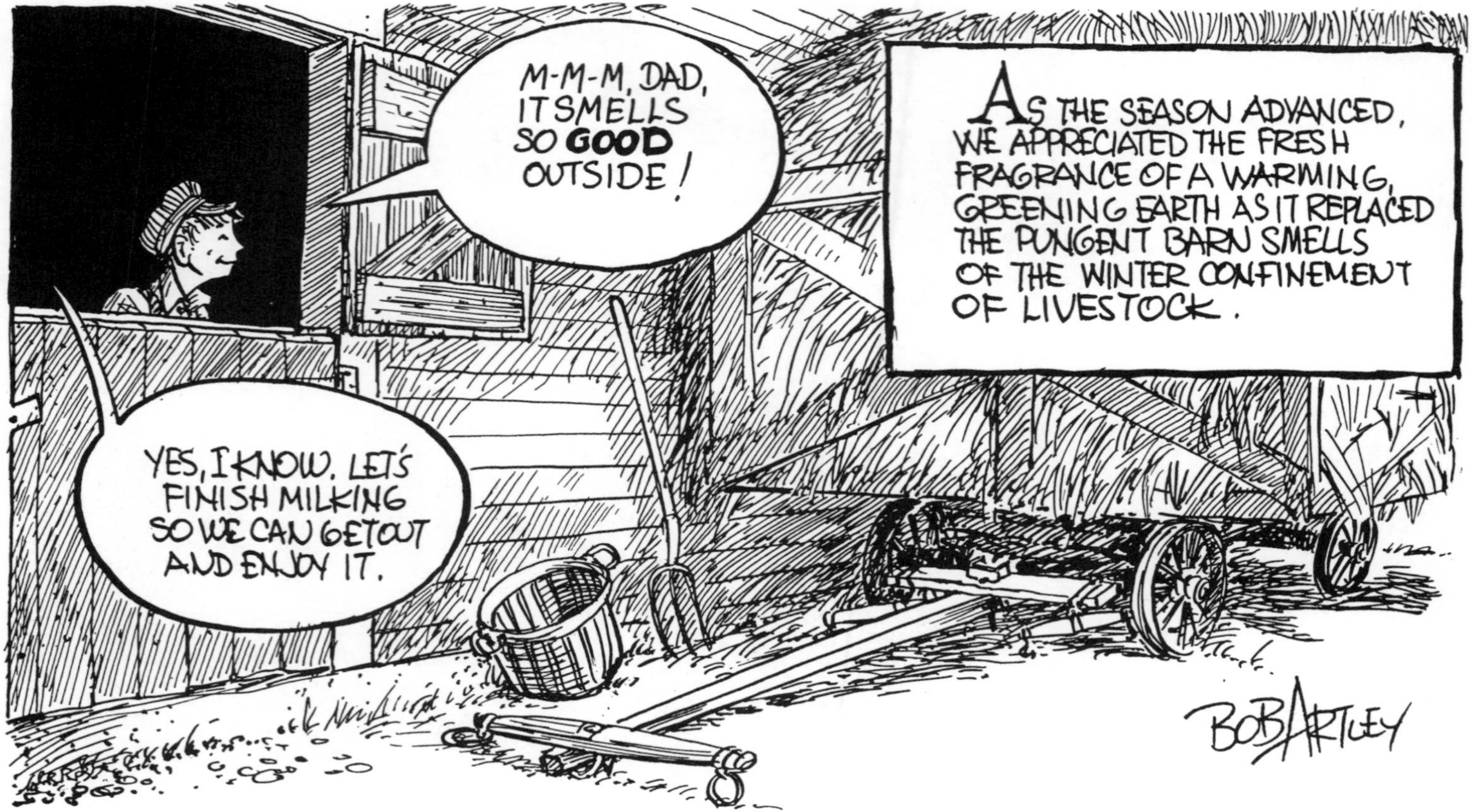
M-M-M, DAD, IT SMELLS SO **GOOD** OUTSIDE!
AS THE SEASON ADVANCED, WE APPRECIATED THE FRESH FRAGRANCE OF A WARMING, GREENING EARTH AS IT REPLACED THE PUNGENT BARN SMELLS OF THE WINTER CONFINEMENT OF LIVESTOCK.
YES, I KNOW. LET'S FINISH MILKING SO WE CAN GET OUT AND ENJOY IT.
BOB ARTLEY

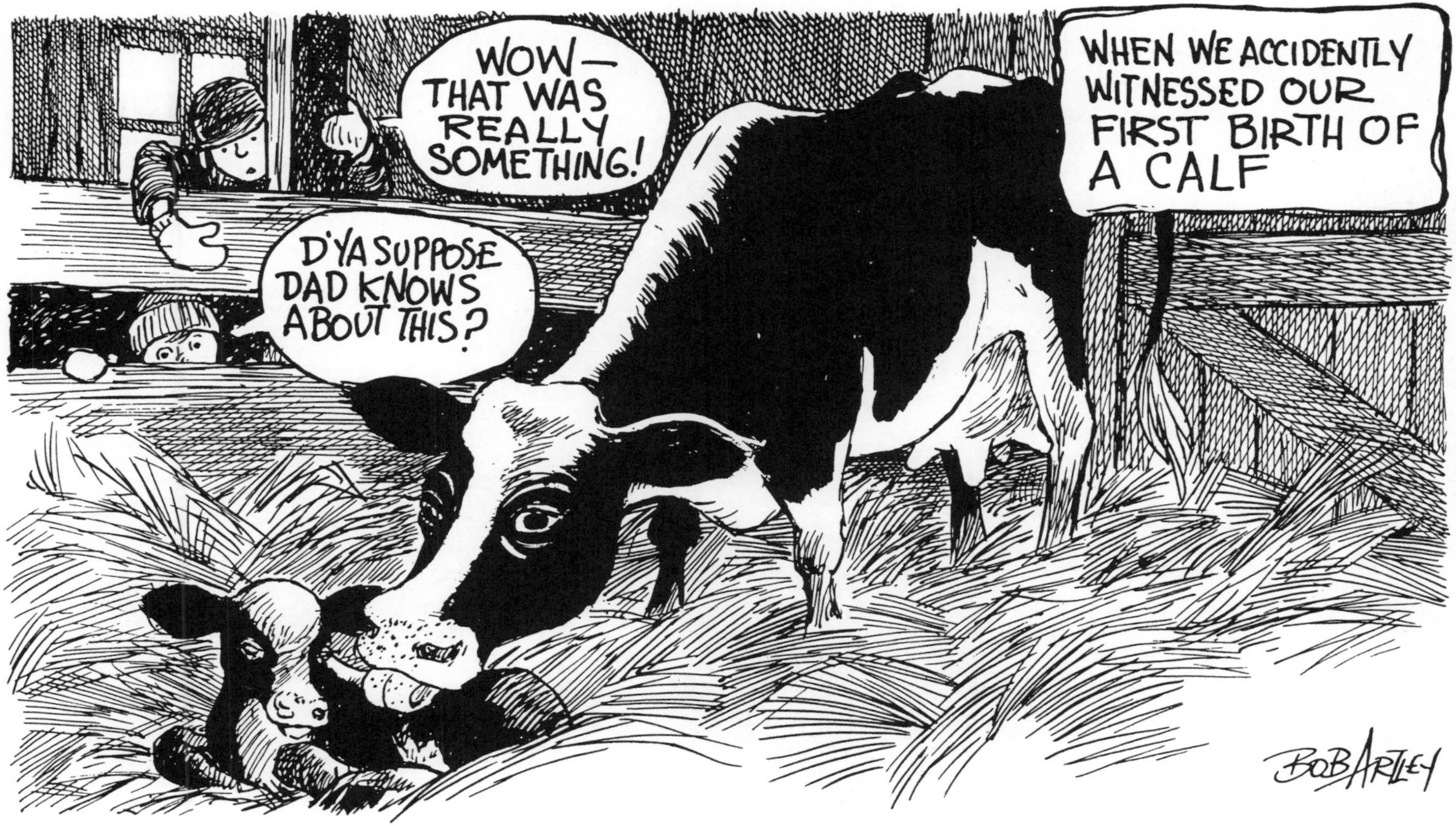
WHEN WE ACCIDENTLY WITNESSED OUR FIRST BIRTH OF A CALF
WOW— THAT WAS REALLY SOMETHING!
D'YA SUPPOSE DAD KNOWS ABOUT THIS?
BOB ARTLEY

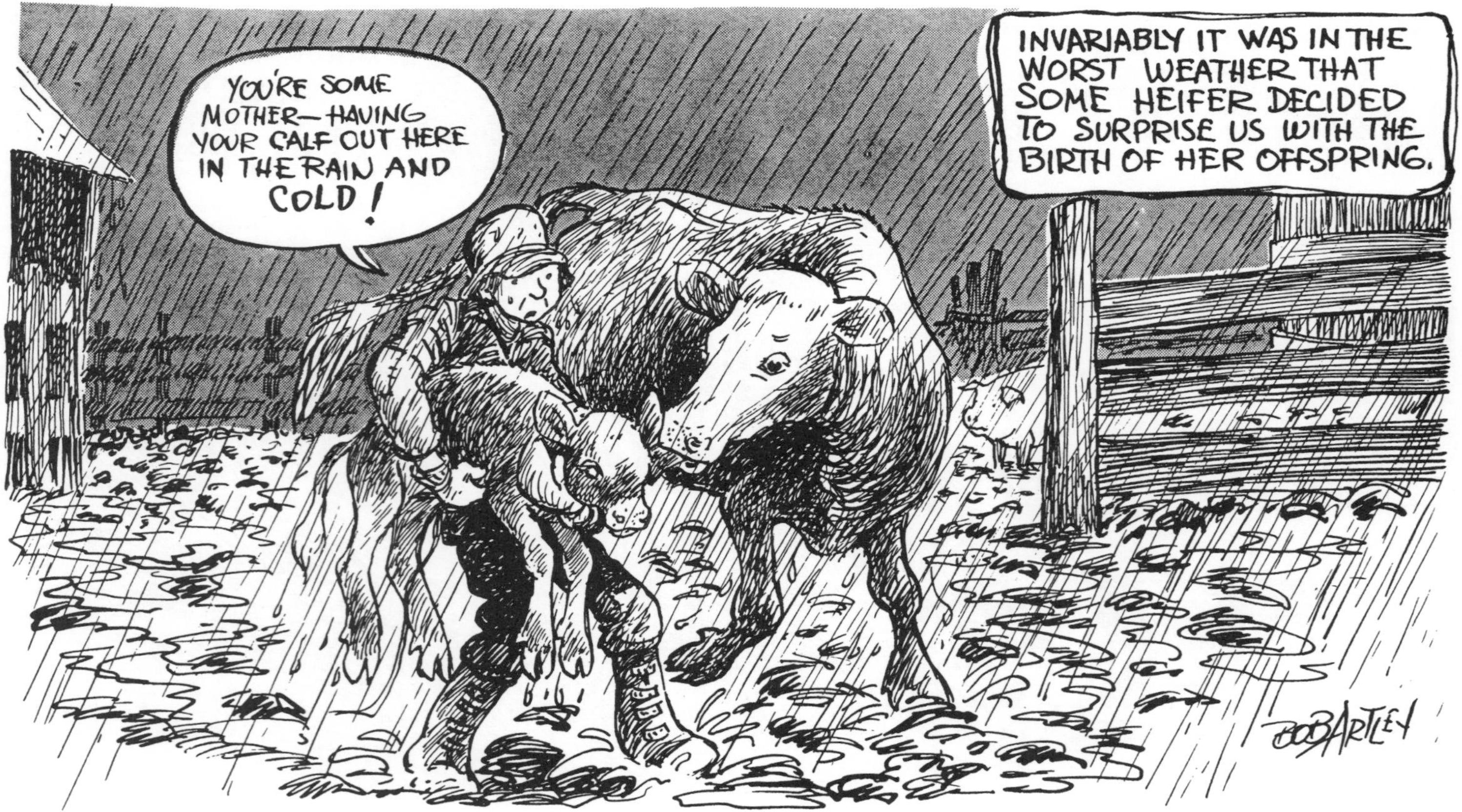
INVARIABLY IT WAS IN THE WORST WEATHER THAT SOME HEIFER DECIDED TO SURPRISE US WITH THE BIRTH OF HER OFFSPRING.
YOU'RE SOME MOTHER— HAVING YOUR CALF OUT HERE IN THE RAIN AND COLD!
BOB BARTLEY

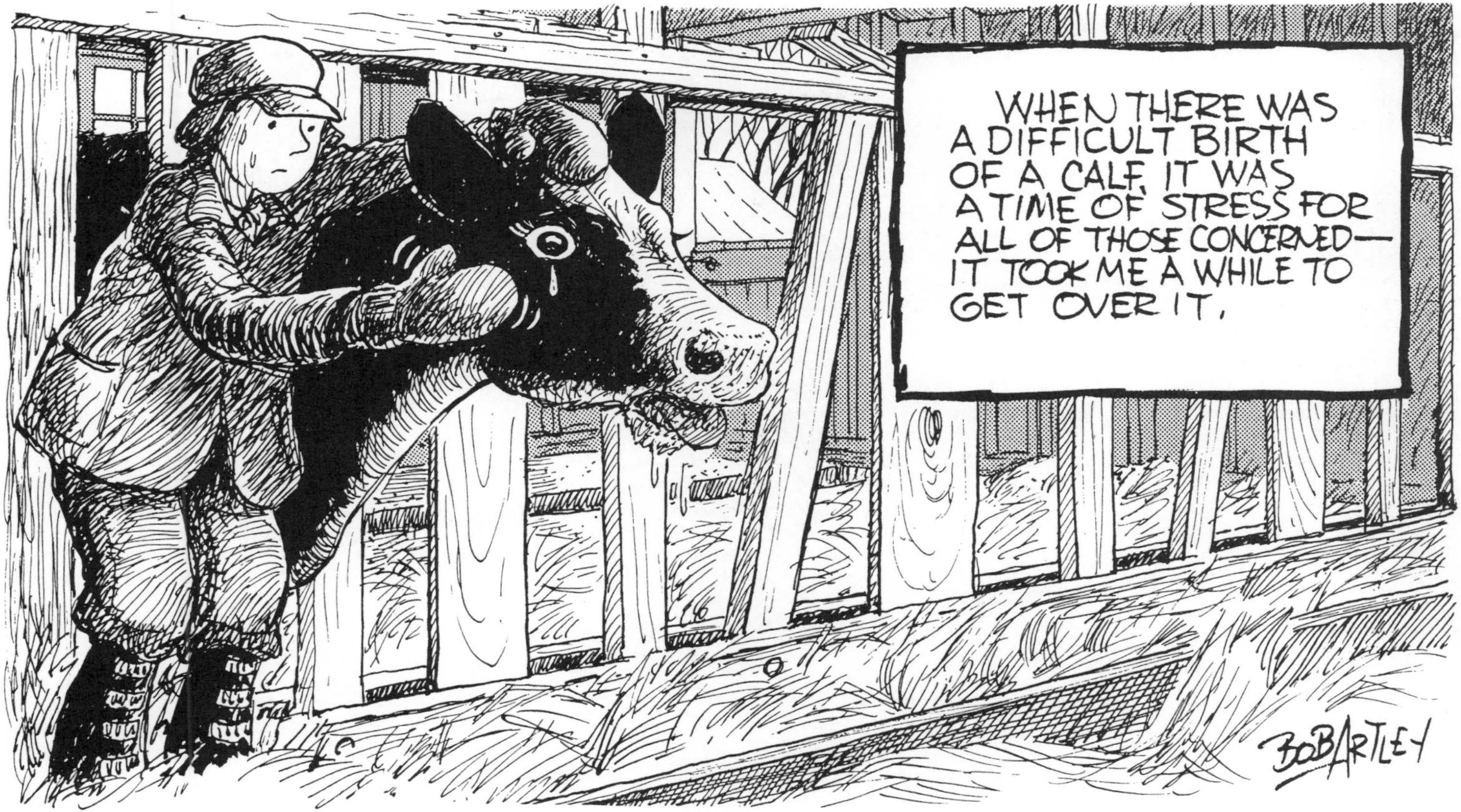
WHEN THERE WAS A DIFFICULT BIRTH OF A CALF, IT WAS A TIME OF STRESS FOR ALL OF THOSE CONCERNED— IT TOOK ME A WHILE TO GET OVER IT.
BOB ARTLEY

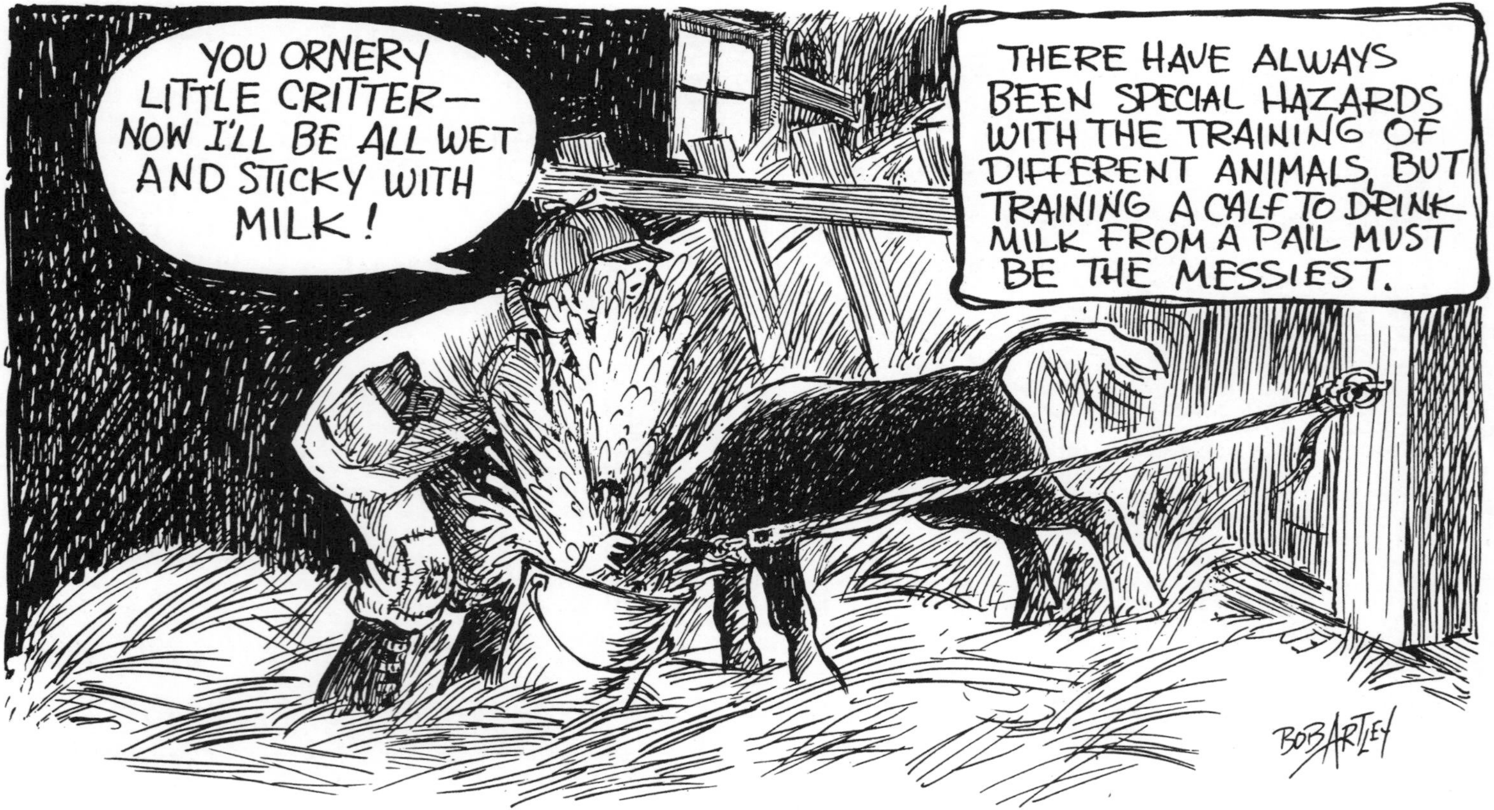
YOU ORNERY LITTLE CRITTER— NOW I'LL BE ALL WET AND STICKY WITH MILK!
THERE HAVE ALWAYS BEEN SPECIAL HAZARDS WITH THE TRAINING OF DIFFERENT ANIMALS, BUT TRAINING A CALF TO DRINK MILK FROM A PAIL MUST BE THE MESSIEST.
BOB ARTLEY

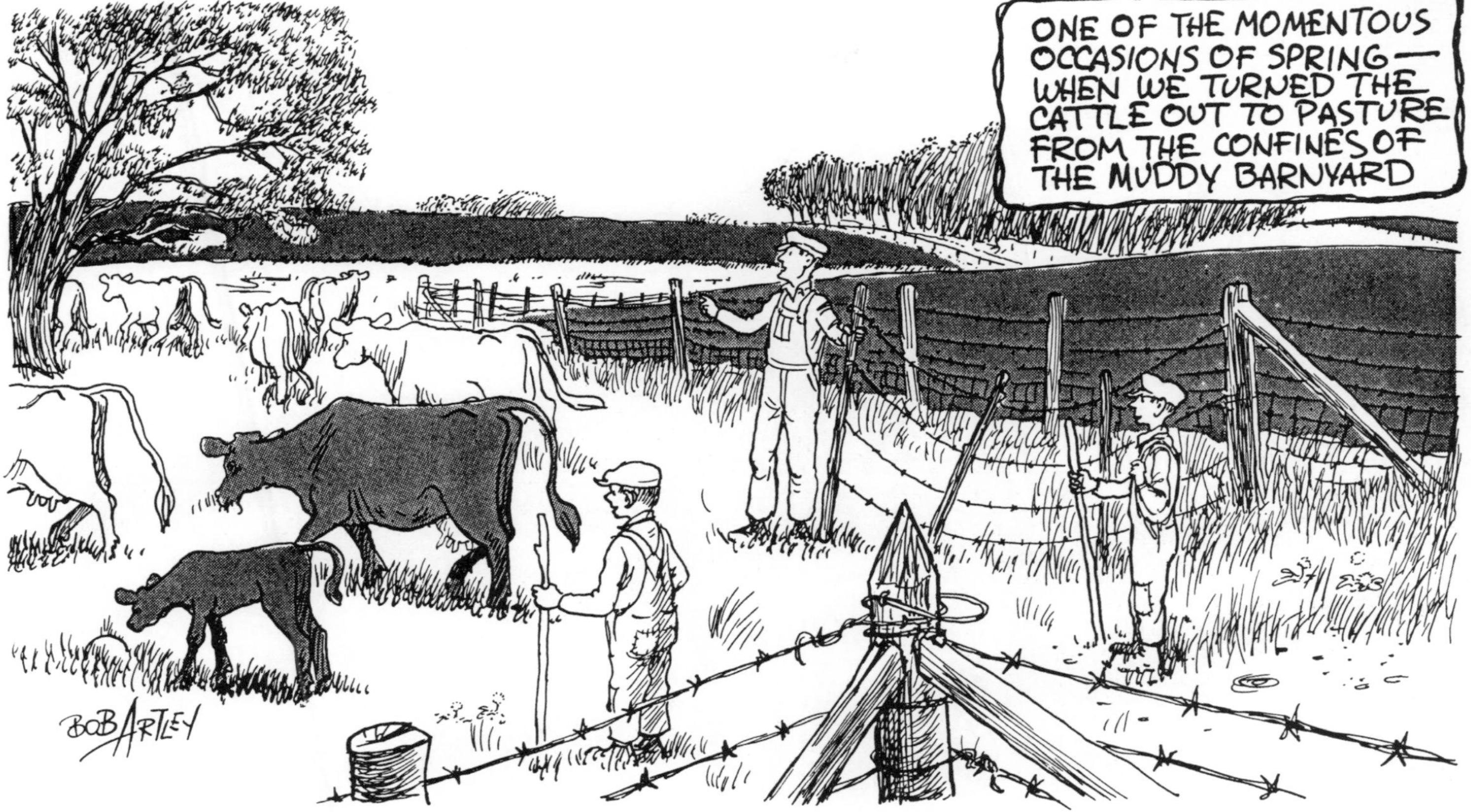
ONE OF THE MOMENTOUS OCCASIONS OF SPRING— WHEN WE TURNED THE CATTLE OUT TO PASTURE FROM THE CONFINES OF THE MUDDY BARNYARD
BOB ARTLEY

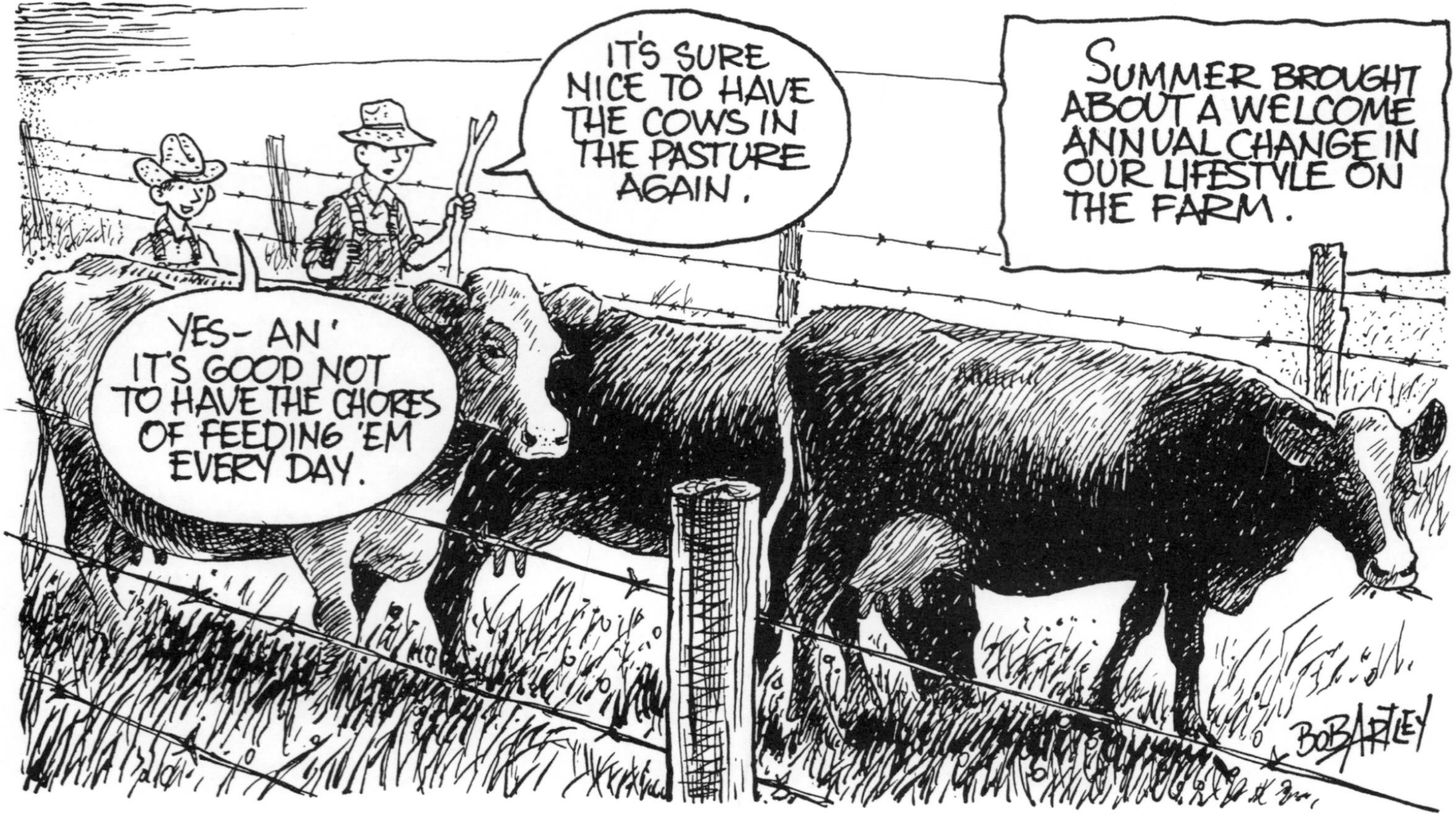
SUMMER BROUGHT ABOUT A WELCOME ANNUAL CHANGE IN OUR LIFESTYLE ON THE FARM.
IT'S SURE NICE TO HAVE THE COWS IN THE PASTURE AGAIN.
YES- AN' IT'S GOOD NOT TO HAVE THE CHORES OF FEEDING 'EM EVERY DAY.
BOB ARTLEY

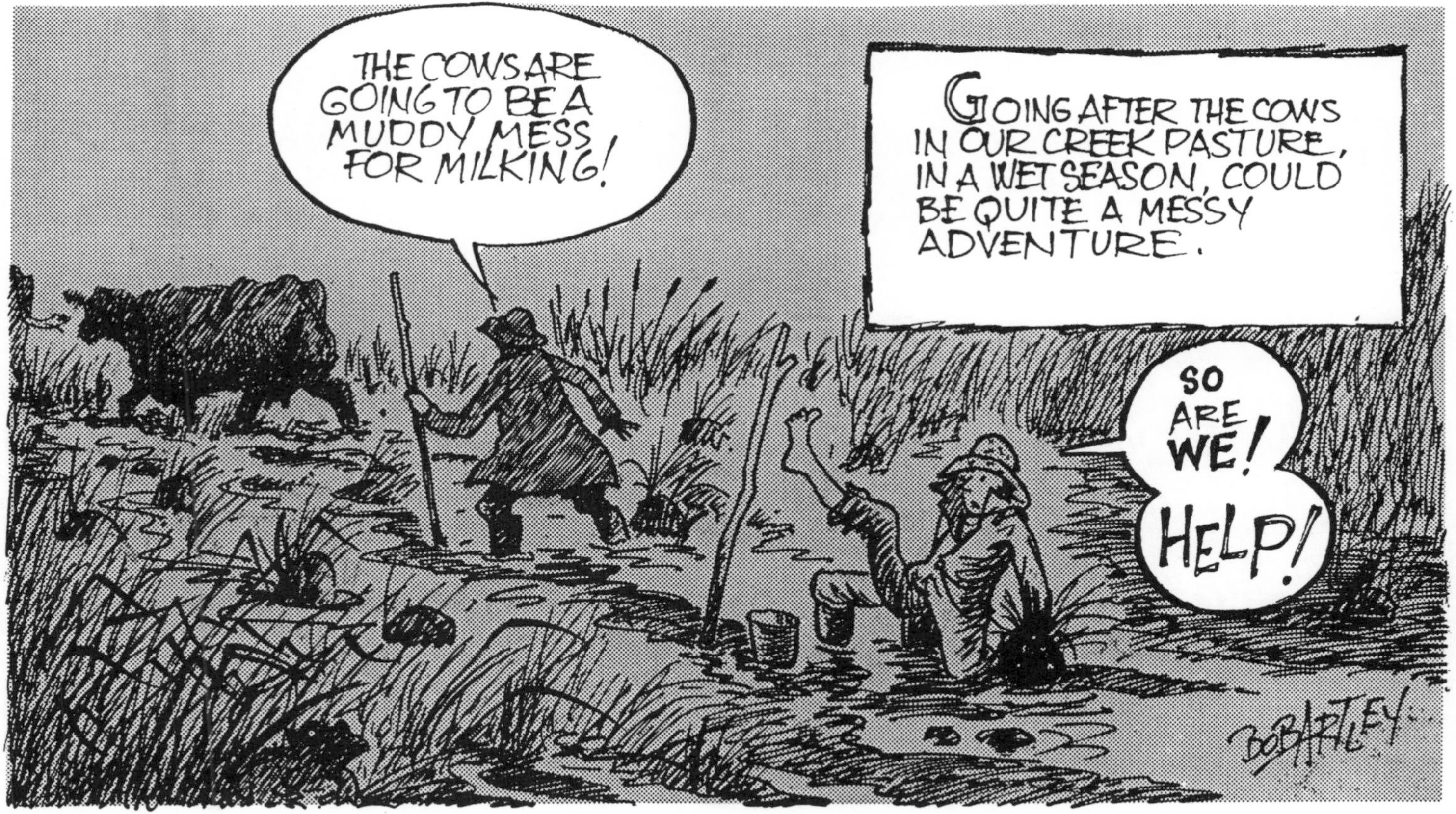
THE COWS ARE GOING TO BE A MUDDY MESS FOR MILKING!
GOING AFTER THE COWS IN OUR CREEK PASTURE, IN A WET SEASON, COULD BE QUITE A MESSY ADVENTURE.
SO ARE WE!
HELP!
BOB ARTLEY

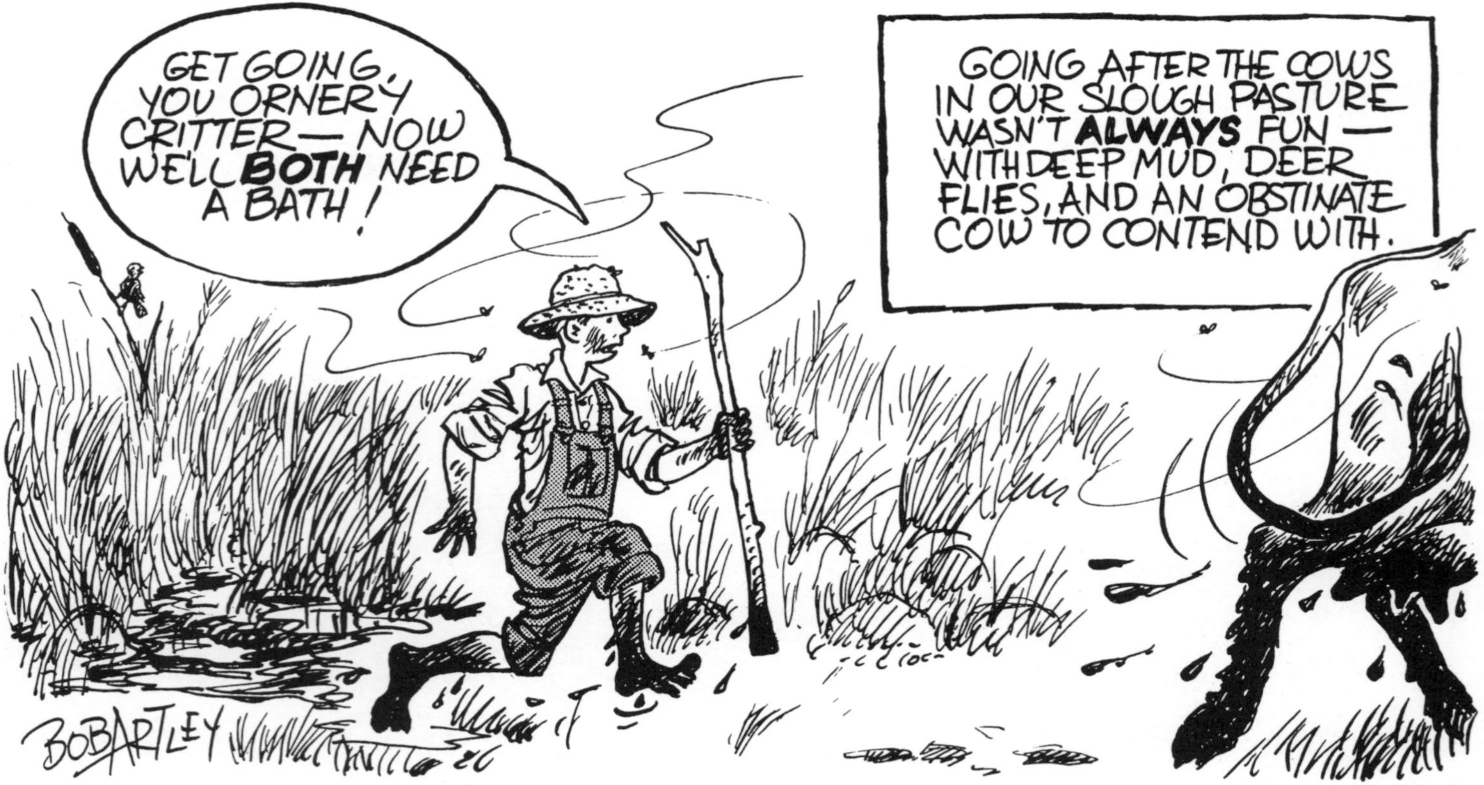
GET GOING, YOU ORNERY CRITTER — NOW WE'LL **BOTH** NEED A BATH!
GOING AFTER THE COWS IN OUR SLOUGH PASTURE WASN'T **ALWAYS** FUN — WITH DEEP MUD, DEER FLIES, AND AN OBSTINATE COW TO CONTEND WITH.
BOB ARTLEY

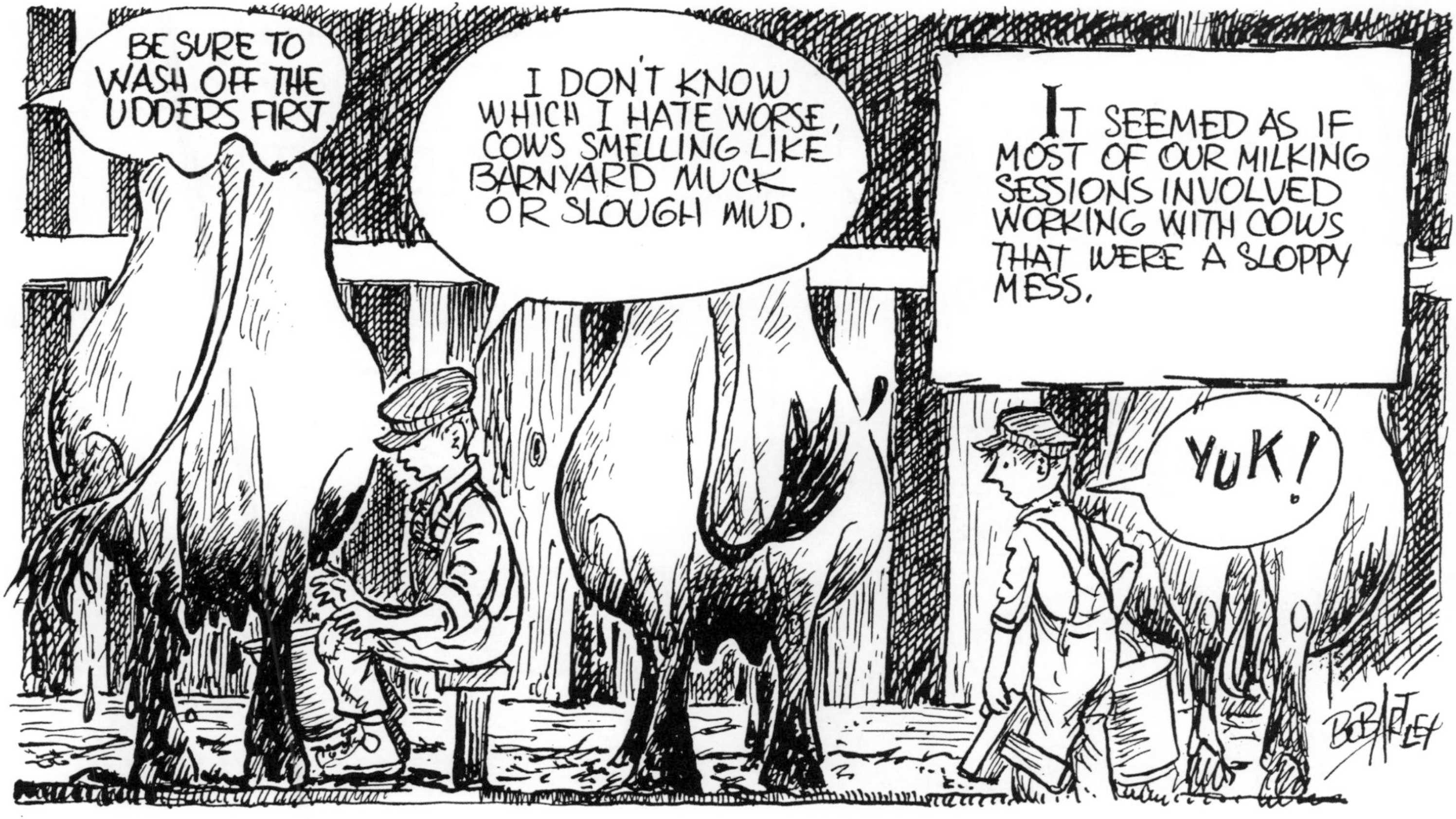
BE SURE TO WASH OFF THE UDDERS FIRST.
I DON'T KNOW WHICH I HATE WORSE, COWS SMELLING LIKE BARNYARD MUCK OR SLOUGH MUD.
IT SEEMED AS IF MOST OF OUR MILKING SESSIONS INVOLVED WORKING WITH COWS THAT WERE A SLOPPY MESS.
YUK!
BOB ARTLEY

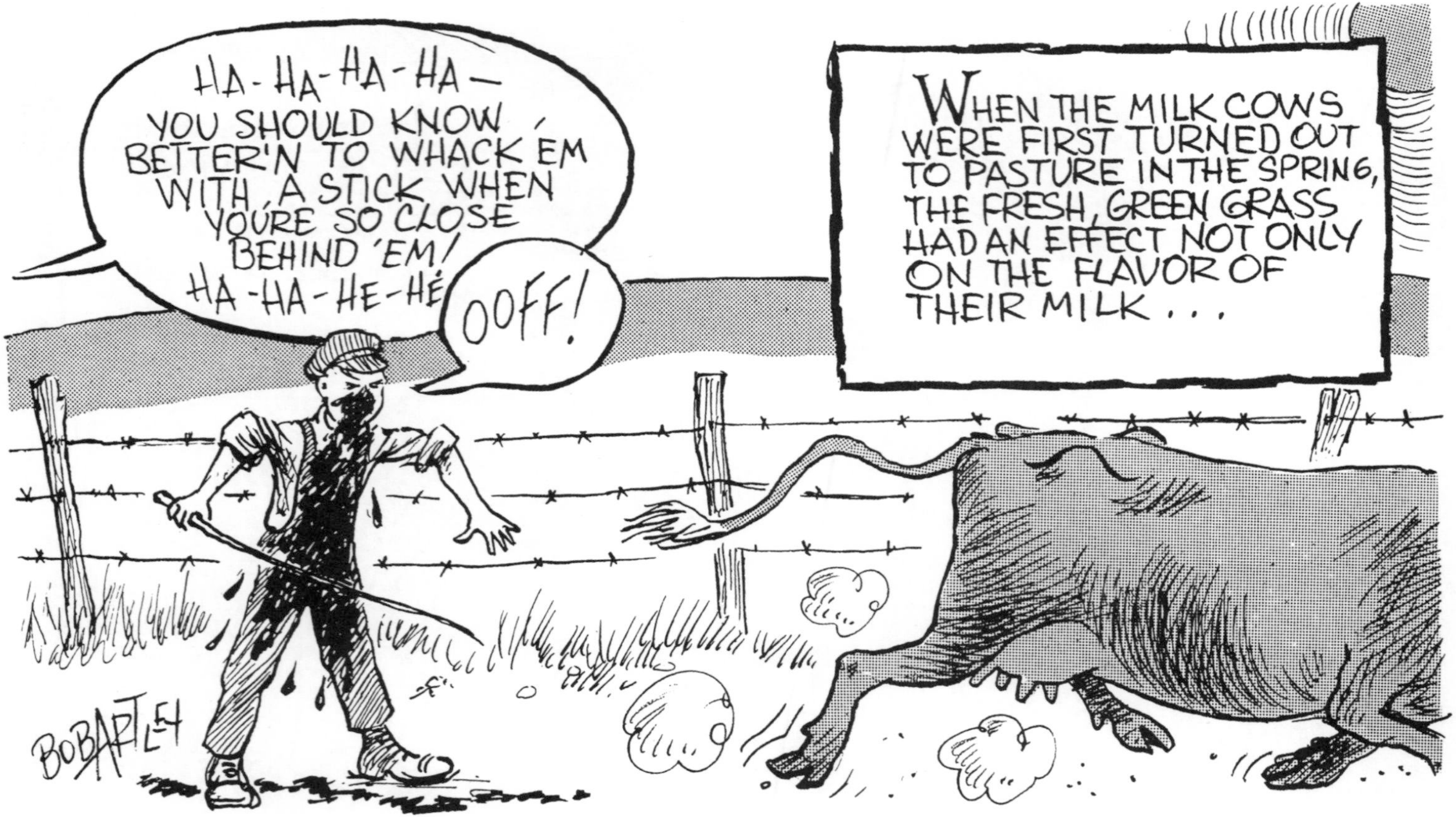
HA-HA-HA-HA— YOU SHOULD KNOW BETTER'N TO WHACK 'EM WITH A STICK WHEN YOU'RE SO CLOSE BEHIND 'EM! HA-HA-HE-HE
OOFF!
WHEN THE MILK COWS WERE FIRST TURNED OUT TO PASTURE IN THE SPRING, THE FRESH, GREEN GRASS HAD AN EFFECT NOT ONLY ON THE FLAVOR OF THEIR MILK . . .
BOB ARTLEY

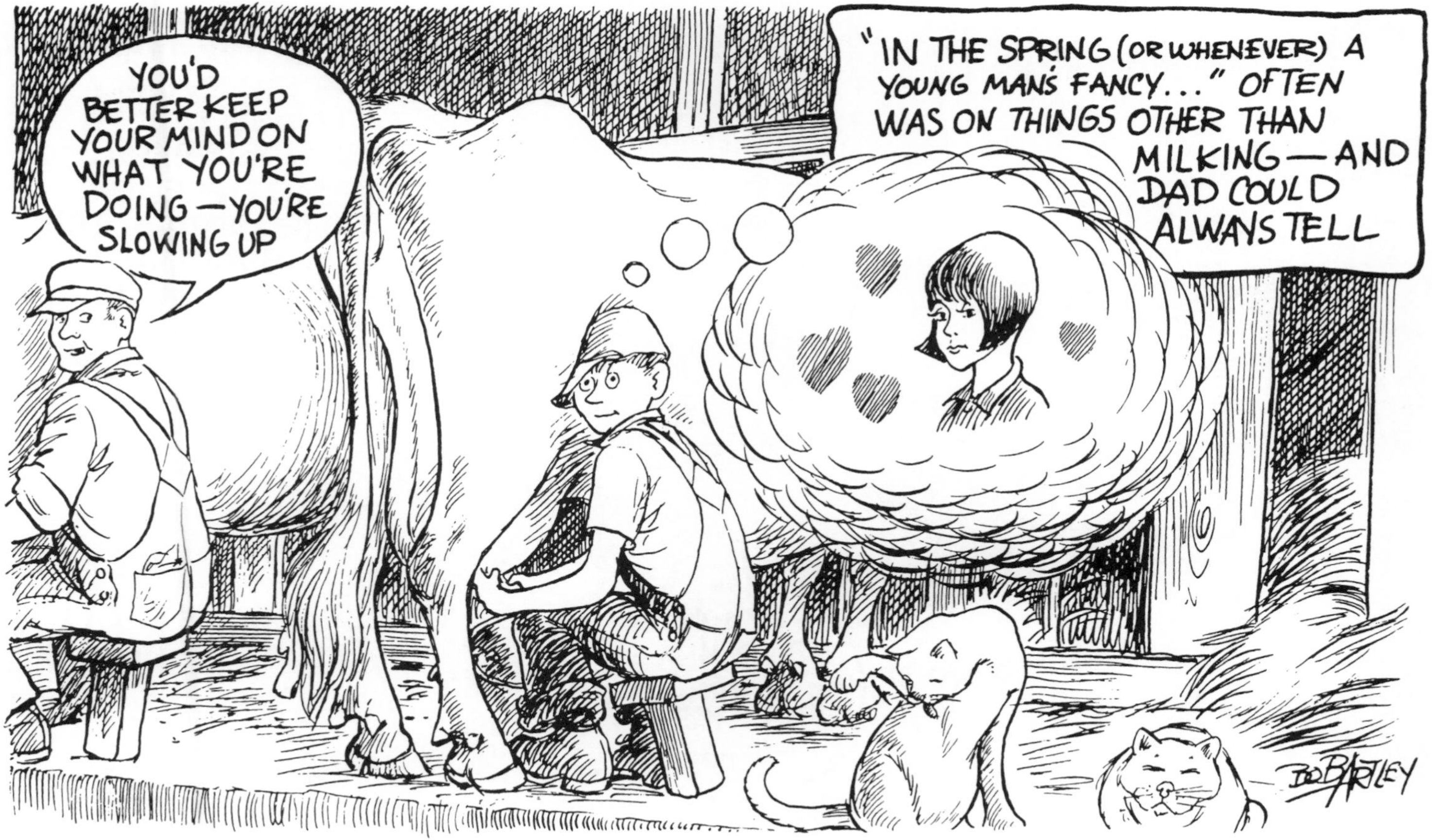
YOU'D BETTER KEEP YOUR MIND ON WHAT YOU'RE DOING — YOU'RE SLOWING UP
"IN THE SPRING (OR WHENEVER) A YOUNG MAN'S FANCY..." OFTEN WAS ON THINGS OTHER THAN MILKING — AND DAD COULD ALWAYS TELL
BOB ARTLEY

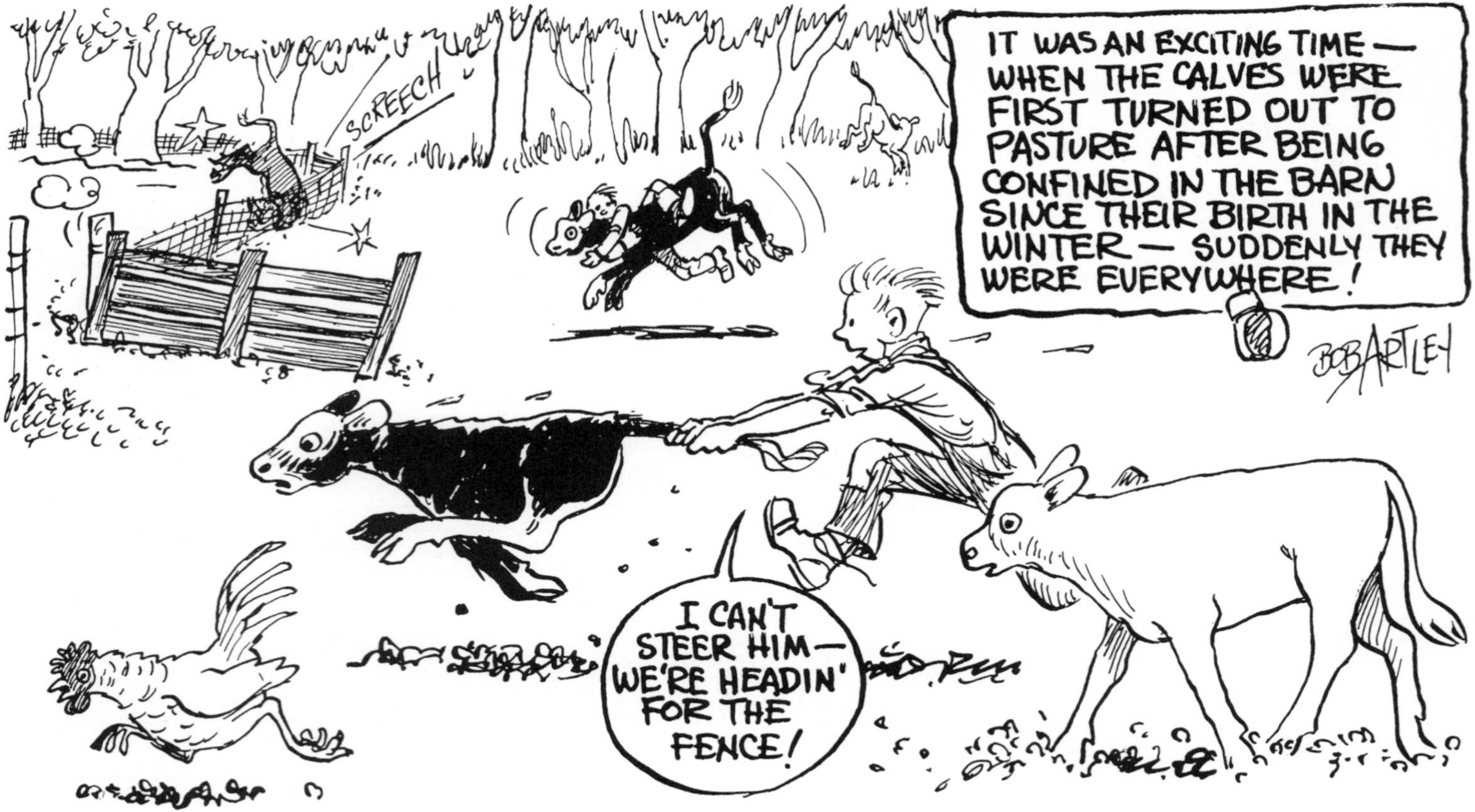
IT WAS AN EXCITING TIME— WHEN THE CALVES WERE FIRST TURNED OUT TO PASTURE AFTER BEING CONFINED IN THE BARN SINCE THEIR BIRTH IN THE WINTER — SUDDENLY THEY WERE EVERYWHERE!
SCREECH
I CAN'T STEER HIM— WE'RE HEADIN' FOR THE FENCE!
BOB ARTLEY

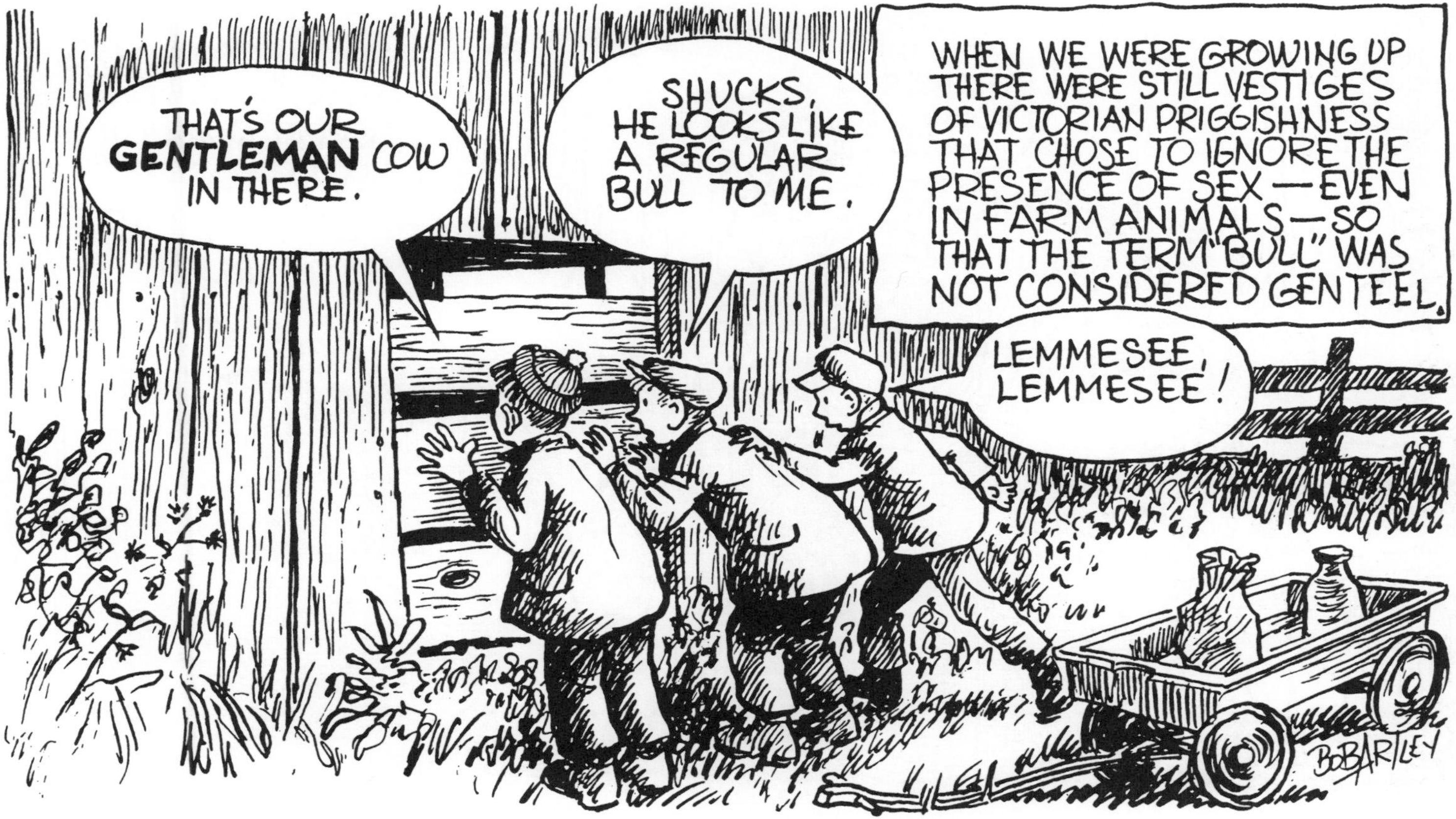
WHEN WE WERE GROWING UP THERE WERE STILL VESTIGES OF VICTORIAN PRIGGISHNESS THAT CHOSE TO IGNORE THE PRESENCE OF SEX — EVEN IN FARM ANIMALS — SO THAT THE TERM "BULL" WAS NOT CONSIDERED GENTEEL.
THAT'S OUR **GENTLEMAN** COW IN THERE.
SHUCKS, HE LOOKS LIKE A REGULAR BULL TO ME.
LEMMESEE, LEMMESEE!
BOB ARTLEY

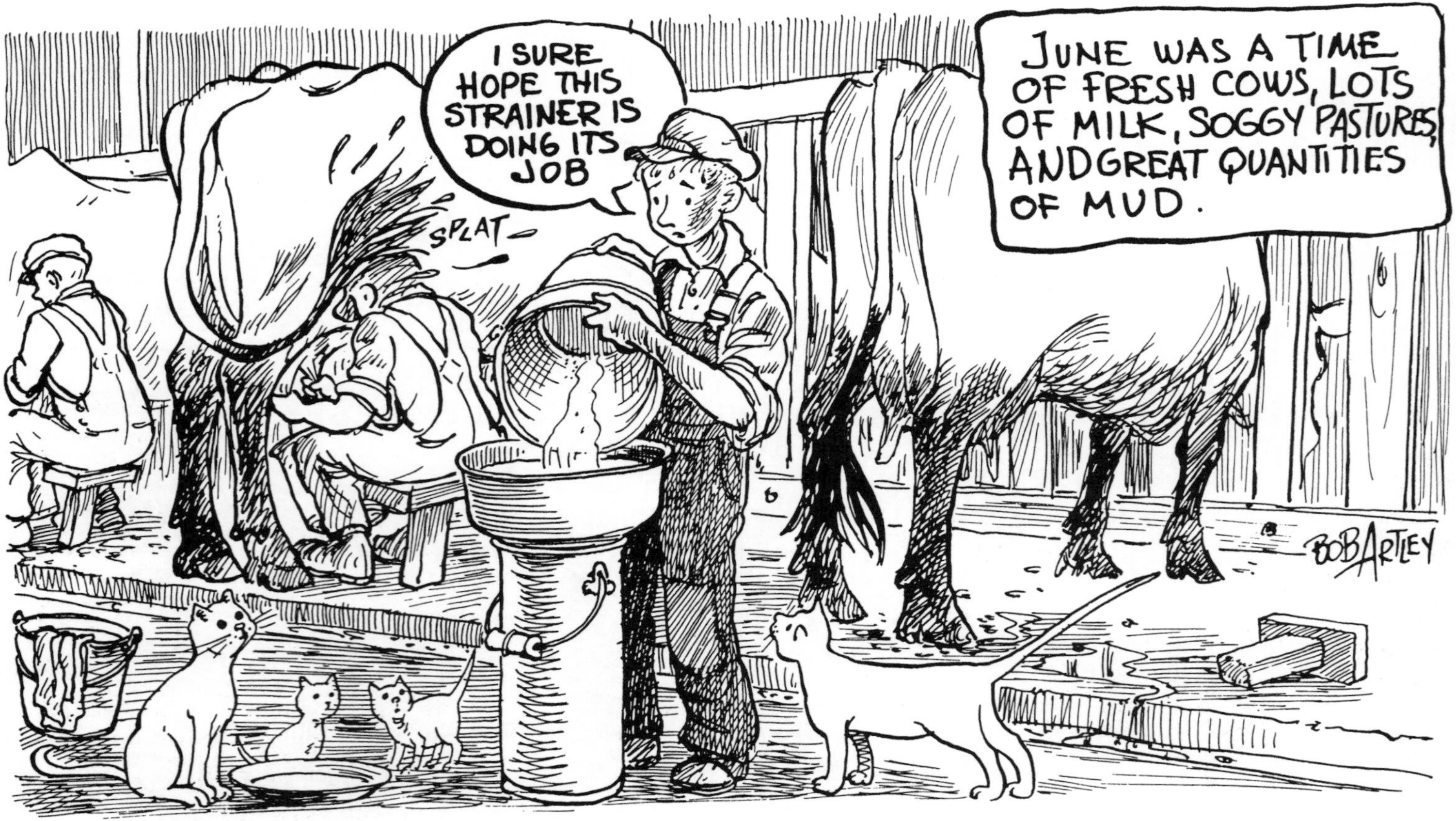
I SURE HOPE THIS STRAINER IS DOING ITS JOB
SPLAT
JUNE WAS A TIME OF FRESH COWS, LOTS OF MILK, SOGGY PASTURES, ANDGREAT QUANTITIES OF MUD.
BOB ARTLEY

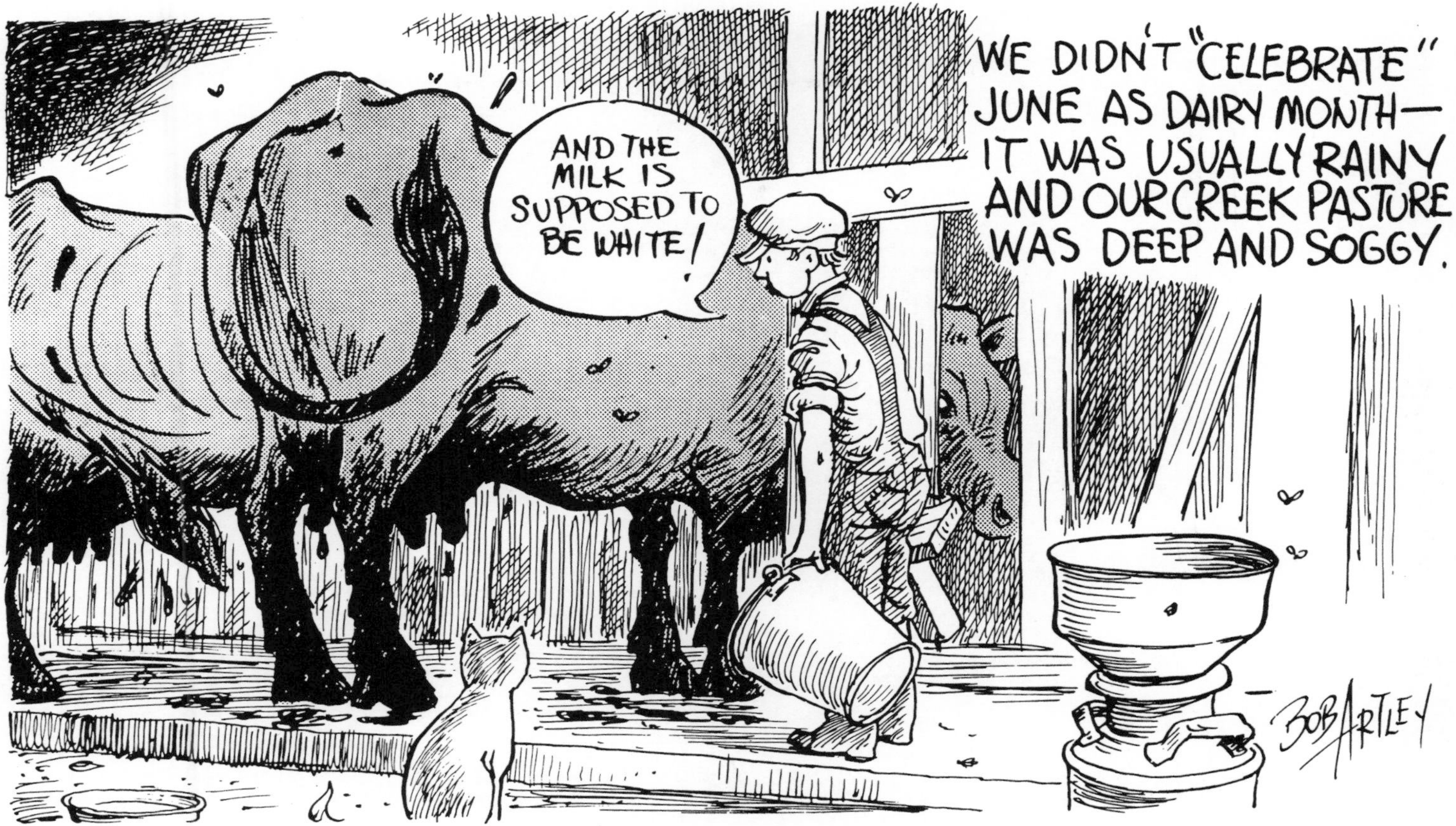

WE DIDN'T "CELEBRATE" JUNE AS DAIRY MONTH— IT WAS USUALLY RAINY AND OUR CREEK PASTURE WAS DEEP AND SOGGY.
AND THE MILK IS SUPPOSED TO BE WHITE!
BOB ARTLEY

Flies

When we were growing up on the farm, the shank of the summer (June, July, and August) was a wonderful time to be alive. But as so often is true of otherwise idyllic conditions, there was "a fly in the ointment."

This spoiler in our Garden of Eden was, to be sure, the fly—or more accurately, flies ... millions of them.

They bred in the ideal environment (for flies) of the manure piles around the barns and the cow patties in the pasture. The flies' eggs hatched into millions of maggots that soon evolved into flies. Even though the free-ranging chickens scratched in these manure piles and fed upon the maggots and grubs they found there, they made no appreciable decrease in the fly population.

One of the great variety of fly species that were generated in these natural incubators was one slightly smaller than a housefly that we called a cowfly. This voracious blood-sucker had a mean bite and was the biggest problem for our bovine co-inhabitants of the cow barn—for cow and herder alike. They covered the backs, sides, bellies, legs, and faces of the poor creatures and made life miserable for them as they bit and sucked their blood.

The only defenses the cows had against their tormentors were their switching tails and to stand in water and mud in close-packed herds.

All of this preoccupation with biting flies cut down on the milk production and could make the process of extracting it a bad experience for cow as well as milker, who had to deal with flailing tails and or kicking hooves.

We tried to mitigate the suffering for all concerned by using various patented fly sprays on the cows when we brought them into the barn, or by wiping them down with a rag soaked in the spray solution. At best, this was only a temporary relief, but it was another incentive (in addition to seeking relief from a full udder) that brought the often stubborn critters into their stanchions willingly.

Mostly, fly time was a time to endure.

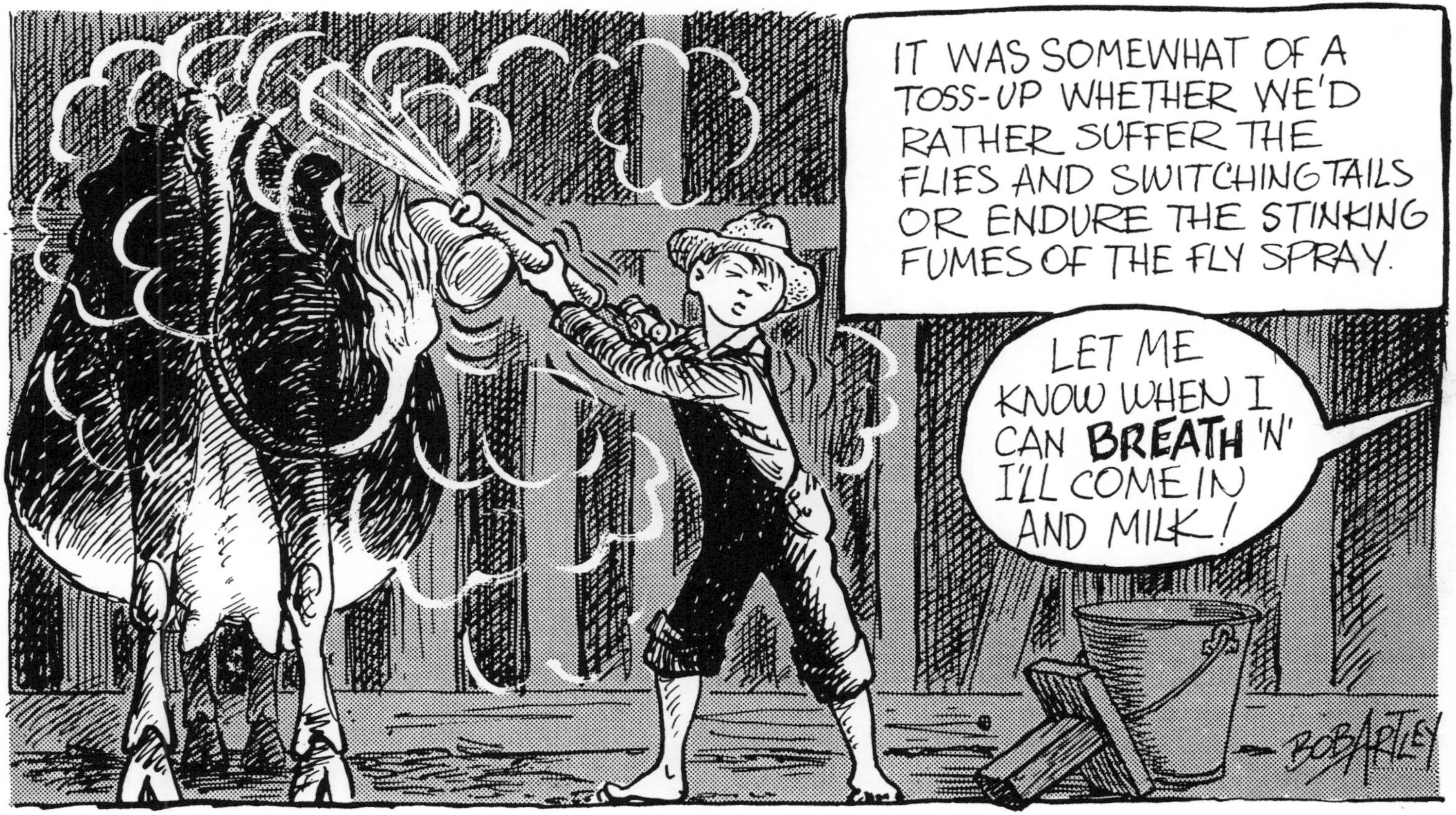
IT WAS SOMEWHAT OF A TOSS-UP WHETHER WE'D RATHER SUFFER THE FLIES AND SWITCHING TAILS OR ENDURE THE STINKING FUMES OF THE FLY SPRAY.
LET ME KNOW WHEN I CAN **BREATH** 'N' I'LL COME IN AND MILK!
BOB ARTLEY

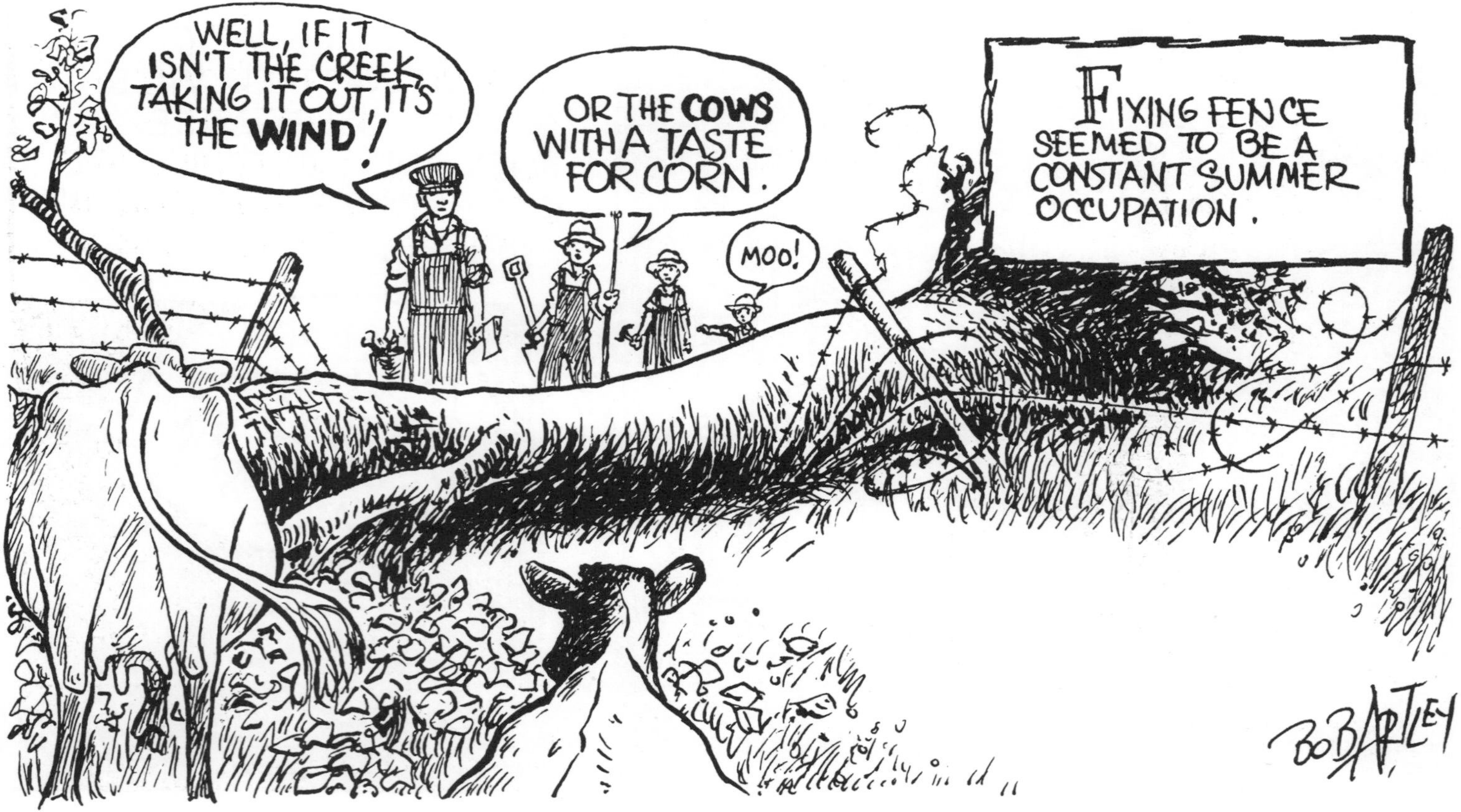
WELL, IF IT ISN'T THE CREEK TAKING IT OUT, IT'S THE **WIND**!
OR THE **COWS** WITH A TASTE FOR CORN.
MOO!
FIXING FENCE SEEMED TO BE A CONSTANT SUMMER OCCUPATION.
BOB ARTLEY

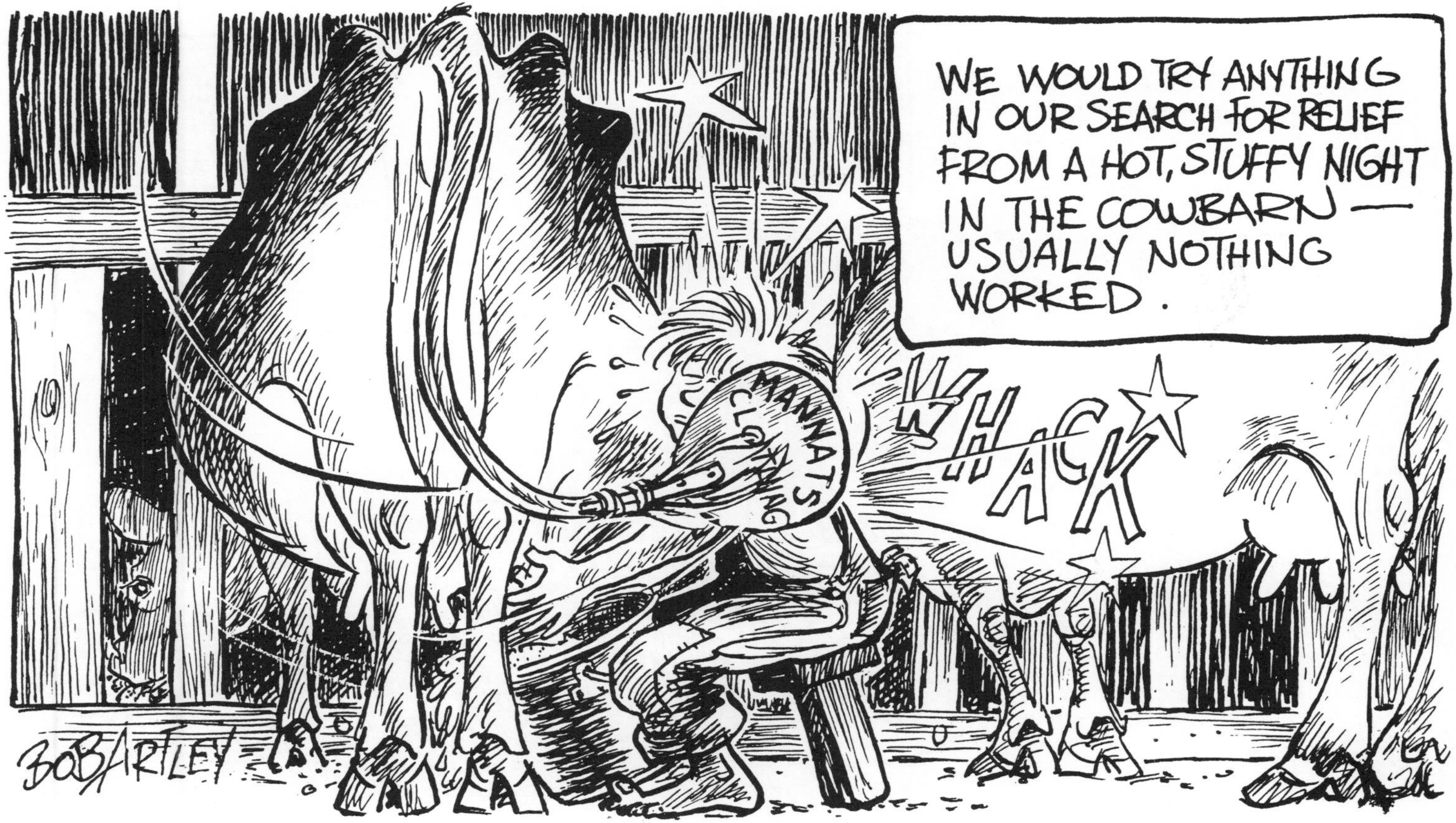
WE WOULD TRY ANYTHING IN OUR SEARCH FOR RELIEF FROM A HOT, STUFFY NIGHT IN THE COWBARN — USUALLY NOTHING WORKED.
MANNATS CLOTHING
WHACK
BOB ARTLEY

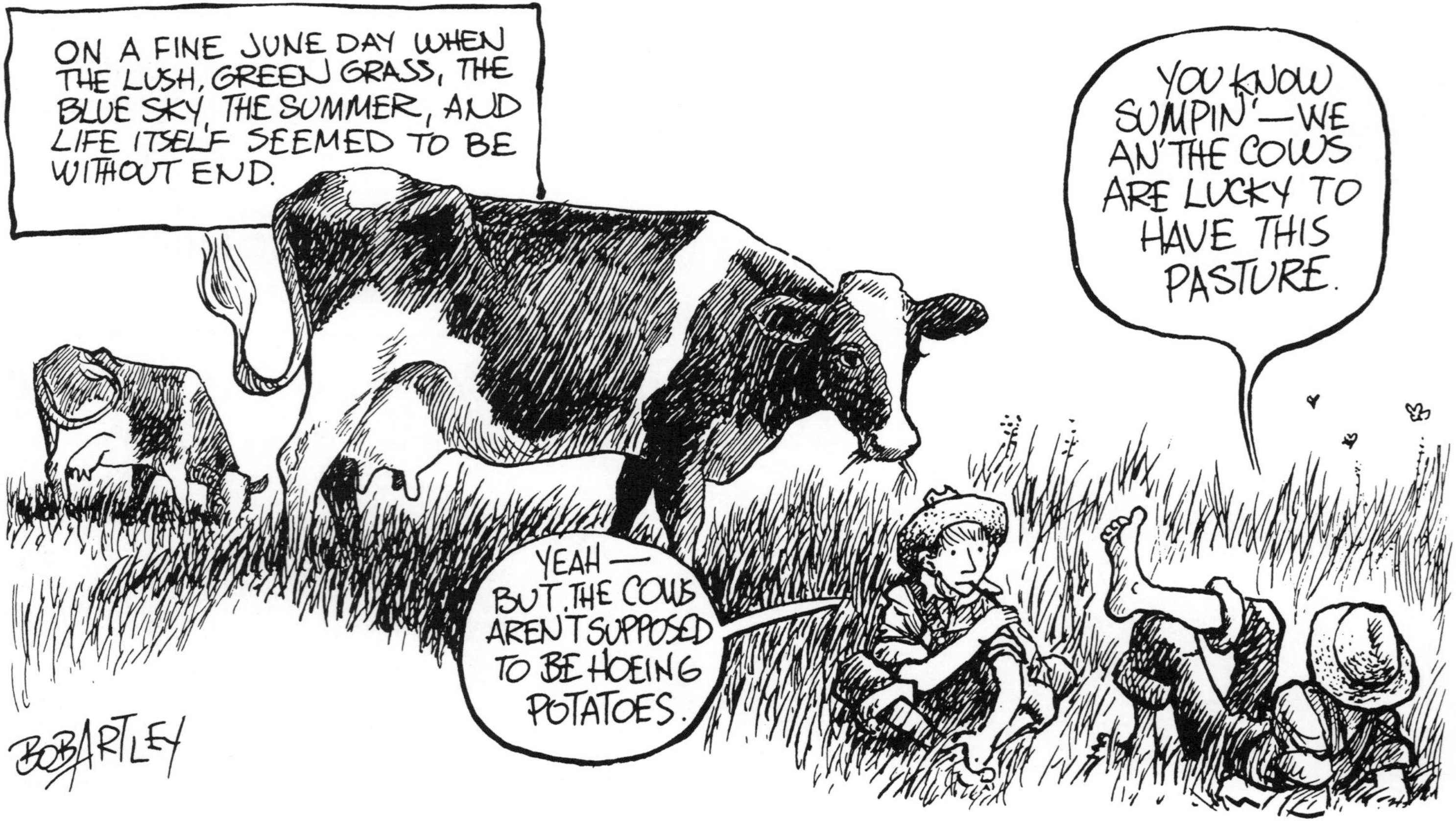
ON A FINE JUNE DAY WHEN THE LUSH, GREEN GRASS, THE BLUE SKY, THE SUMMER, AND LIFE ITSELF SEEMED TO BE WITHOUT END.
YOU KNOW SUMPIN'—WE AN' THE COWS ARE LUCKY TO HAVE THIS PASTURE.
YEAH — BUT THE COWS AREN'T SUPPOSED TO BE HOEING POTATOES.
BOB ARTLEY

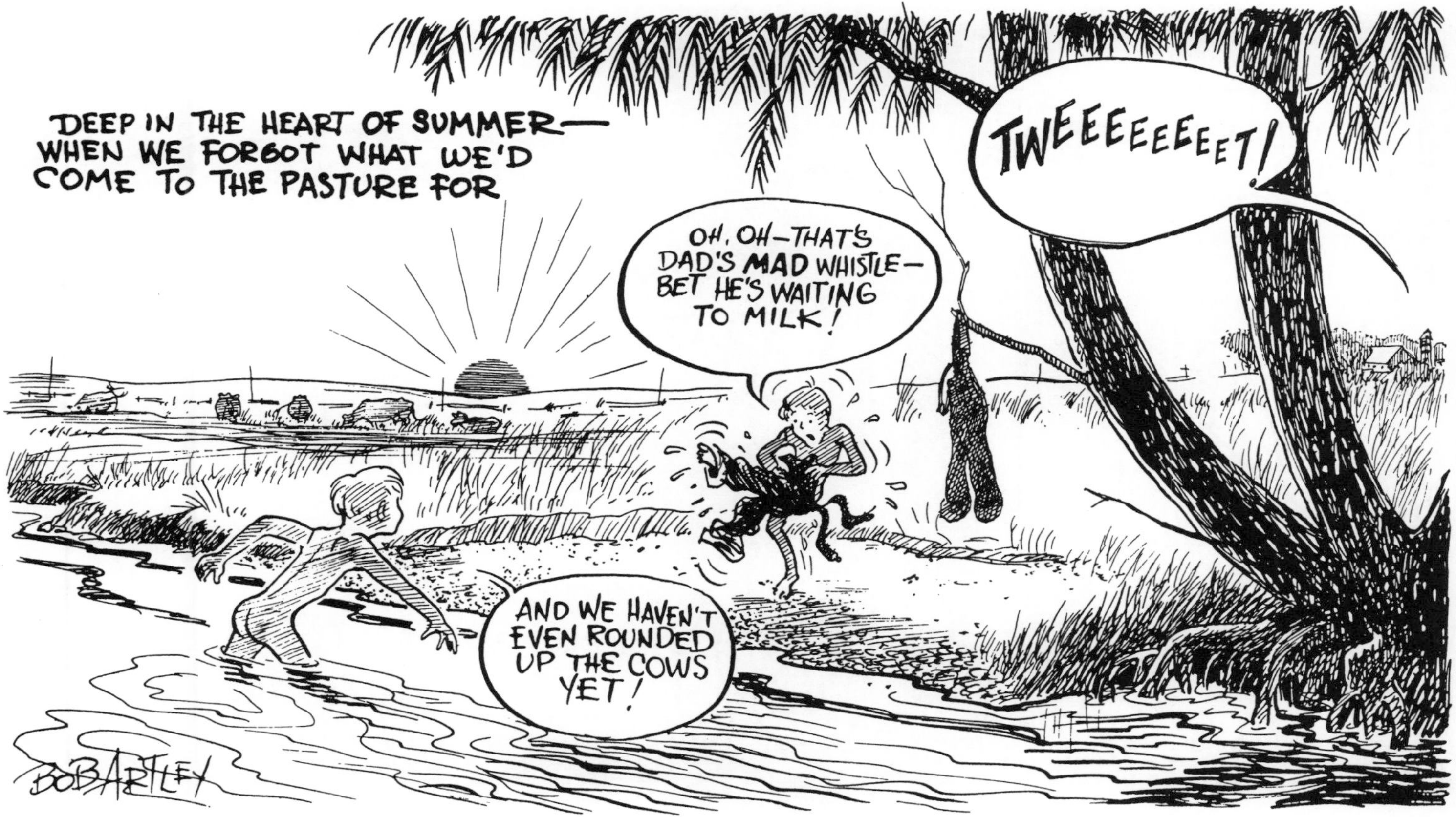
DEEP IN THE HEART OF SUMMER— WHEN WE FORGOT WHAT WE'D COME TO THE PASTURE FOR
TWEEEEEEEEET!
OH, OH—THAT'S DAD'S MAD WHISTLE— BET HE'S WAITING TO MILK!
AND WE HAVEN'T EVEN ROUNDED UP THE COWS YET!
BOB ARTLEY

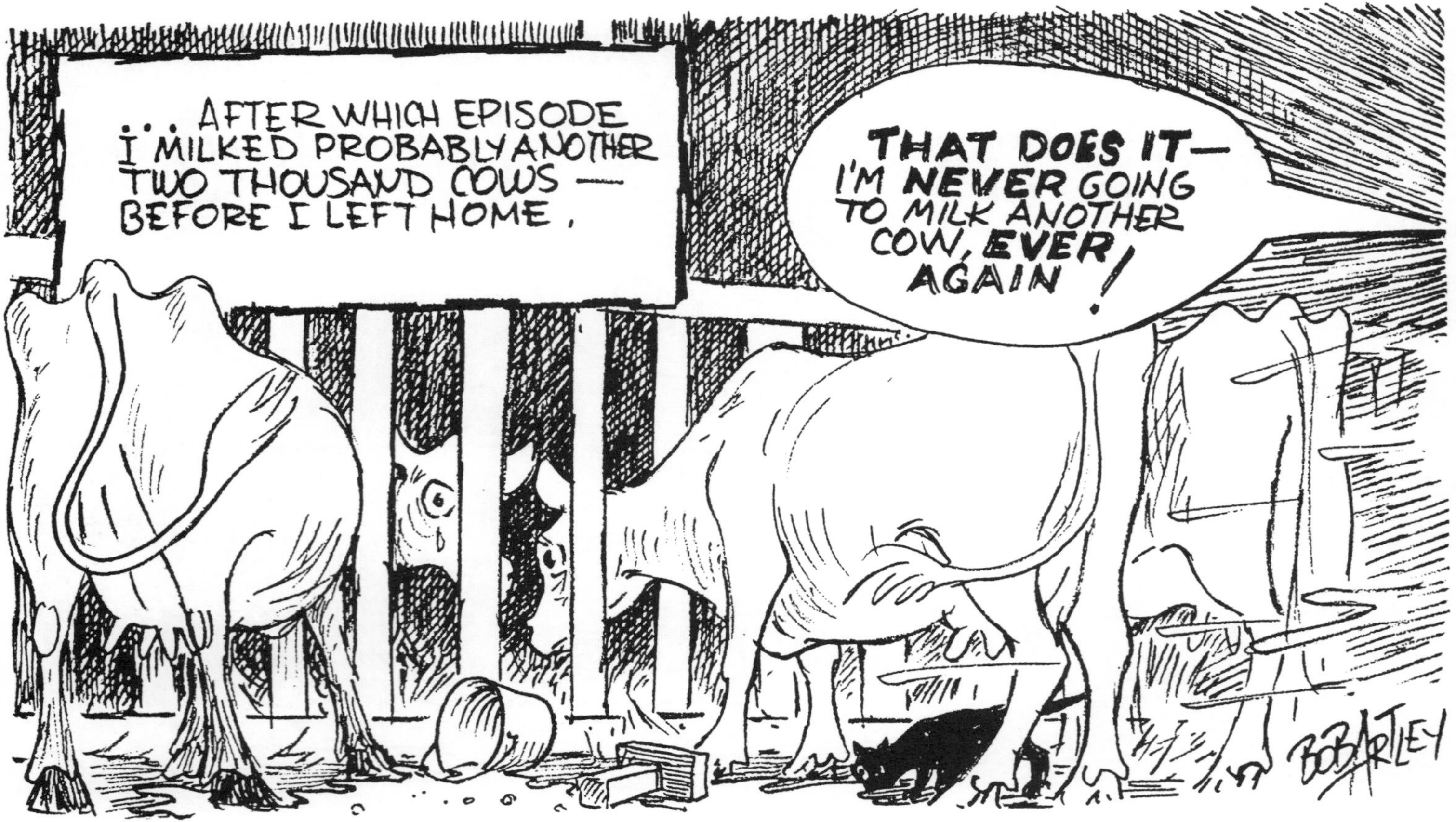

... AFTER WHICH EPISODE I MILKED PROBABLY ANOTHER TWO THOUSAND COWS — BEFORE I LEFT HOME.
THAT DOES IT— I'M NEVER GOING TO MILK ANOTHER COW, EVER AGAIN!
BOB BARTLEY

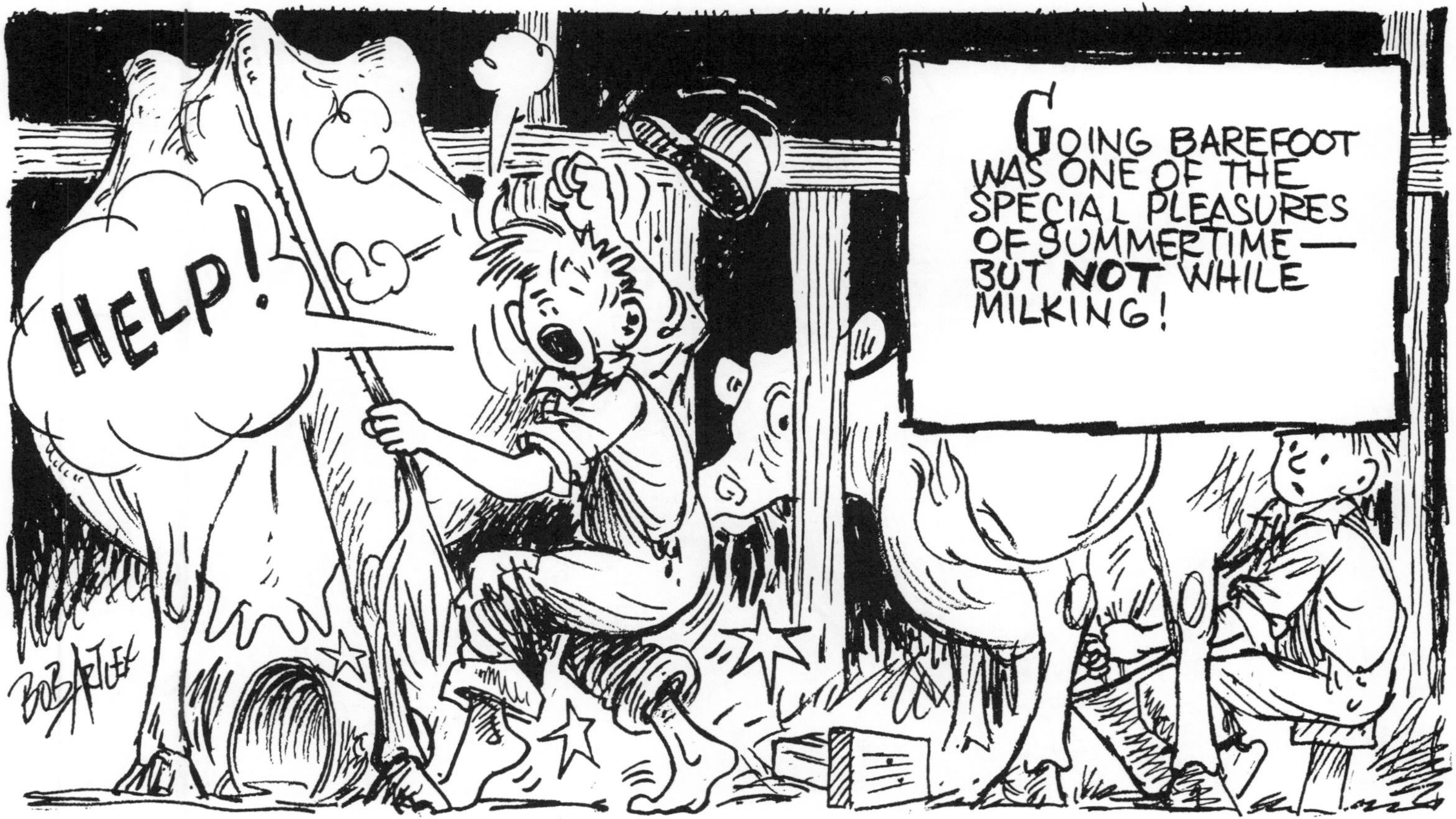
HELP!
GOING BAREFOOT WAS ONE OF THE SPECIAL PLEASURES OF SUMMERTIME— BUT NOT WHILE MILKING!
BOB ARTLEY

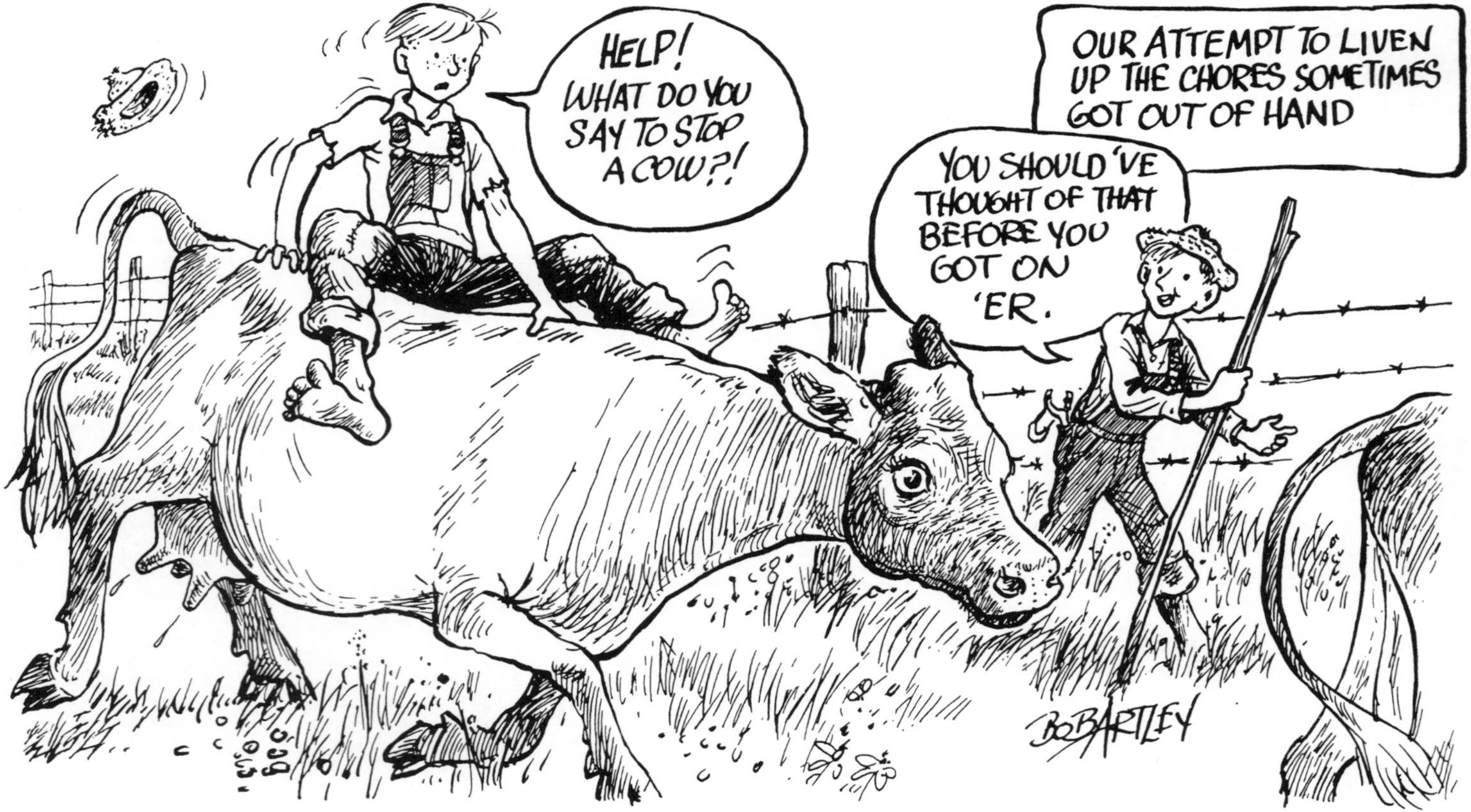
OUR ATTEMPT TO LIVEN UP THE CHORES SOMETIMES GOT OUT OF HAND
HELP! WHAT DO YOU SAY TO STOP A COW?!
YOU SHOULD 'VE THOUGHT OF THAT BEFORE YOU GOT ON 'ER.
BO BARTLEY

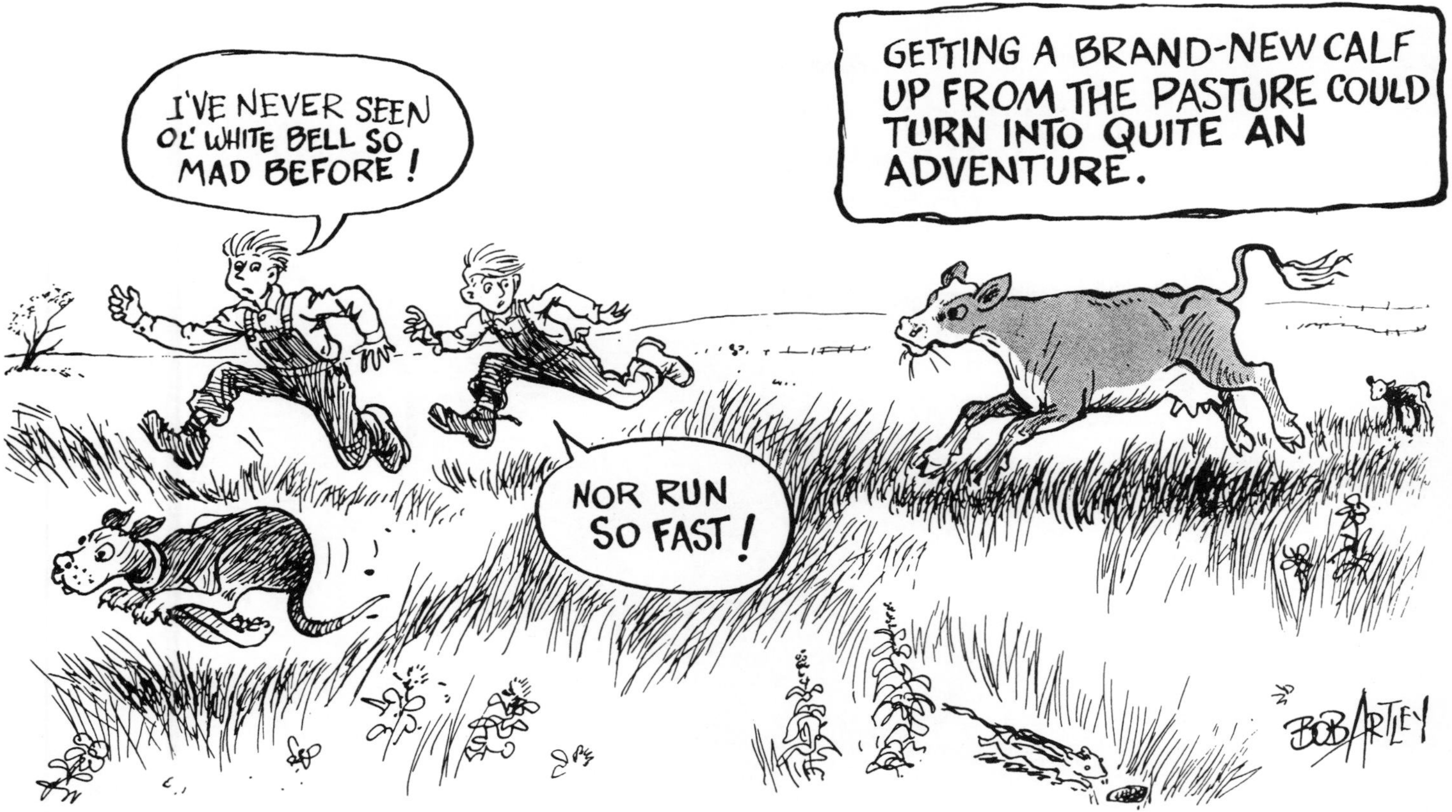
GETTING A BRAND-NEW CALF UP FROM THE PASTURE COULD TURN INTO QUITE AN ADVENTURE.
I'VE NEVER SEEN OL' WHITE BELL SO MAD BEFORE!
NOR RUN SO FAST!
BOB ARTLEY

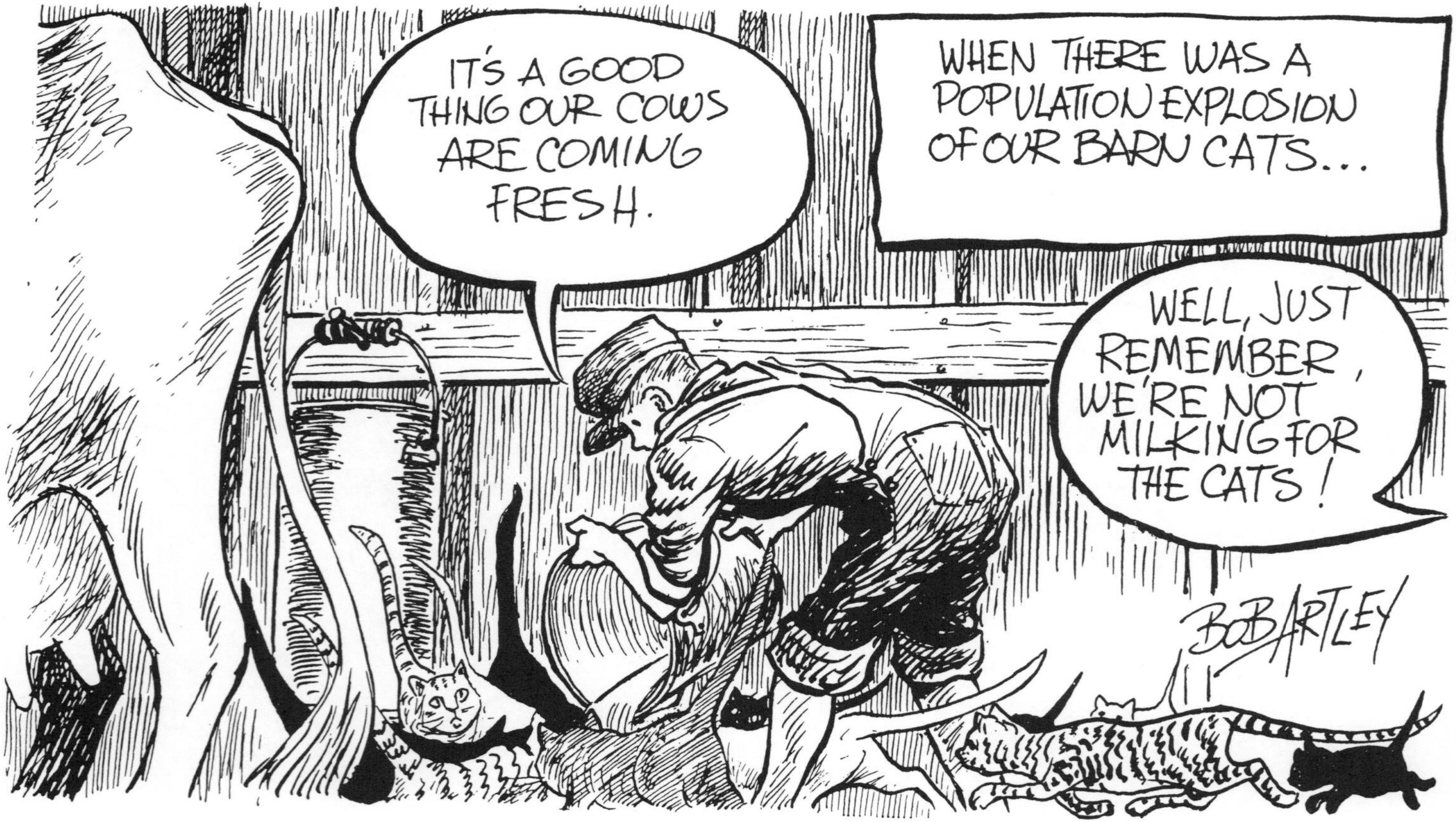
WHEN THERE WAS A POPULATION EXPLOSION OF OUR BARN CATS...
IT'S A GOOD THING OUR COWS ARE COMING FRESH.
WELL, JUST REMEMBER, WE'RE NOT MILKING FOR THE CATS!
BOB ARTLEY

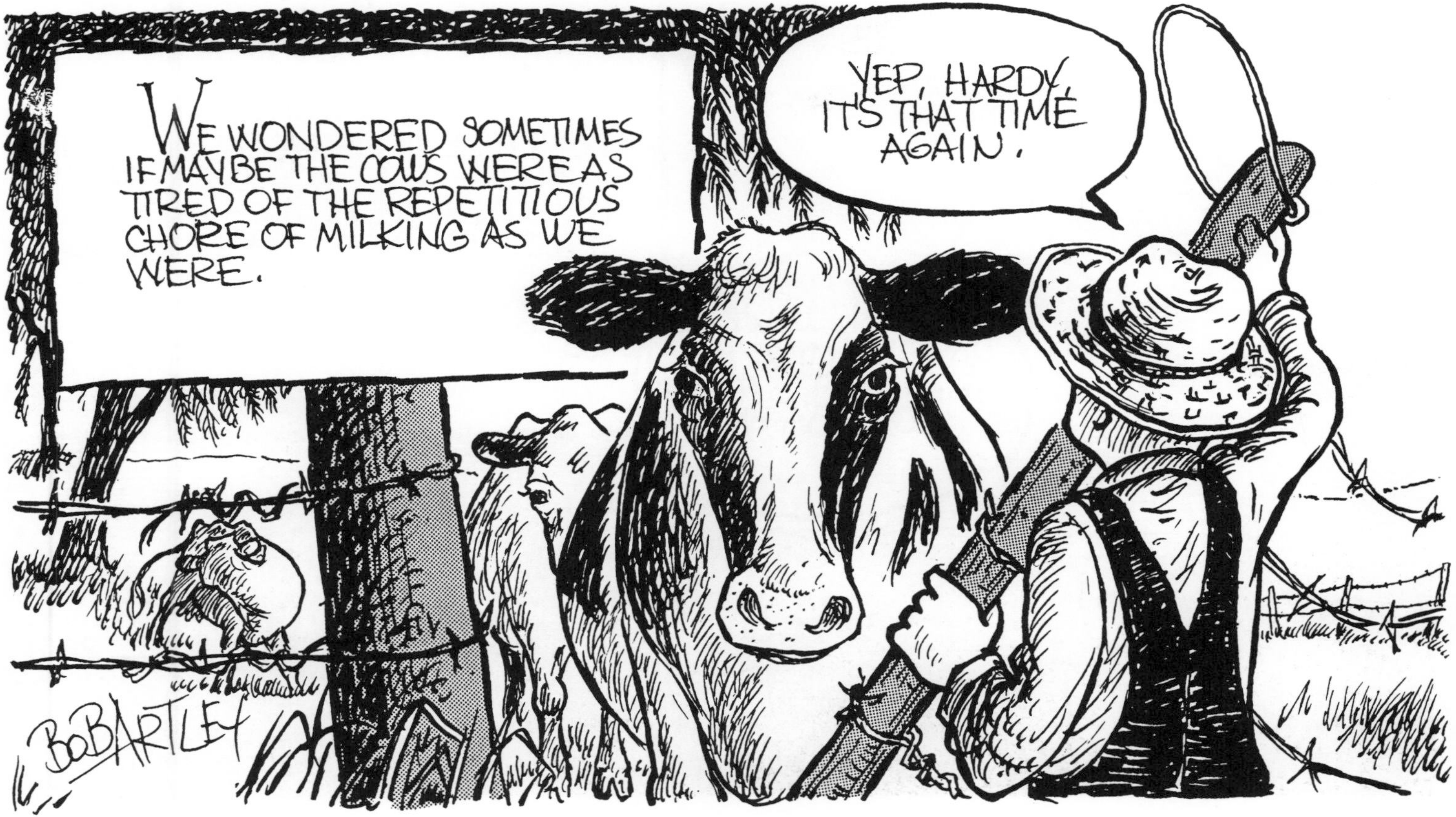
WE WONDERED SOMETIMES IF MAYBE THE COWS WERE AS TIRED OF THE REPETITIOUS CHORE OF MILKING AS WE WERE.
YEP, HARDY, IT'S THAT TIME AGAIN.
BOB BARTLEY

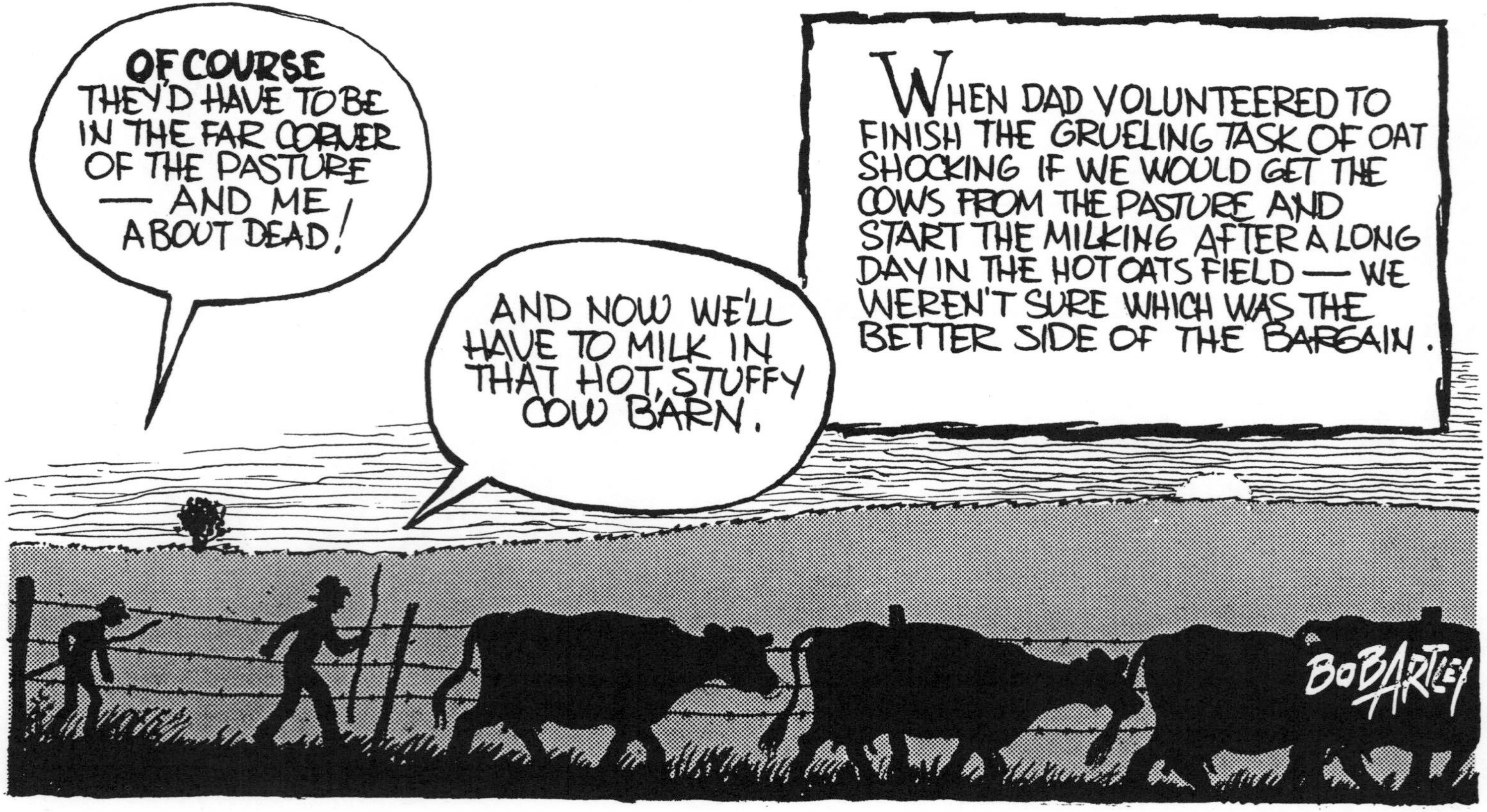
WHEN DAD VOLUNTEERED TO FINISH THE GRUELING TASK OF OAT SHOCKING IF WE WOULD GET THE COWS FROM THE PASTURE AND START THE MILKING AFTER A LONG DAY IN THE HOT OATS FIELD — WE WEREN'T SURE WHICH WAS THE BETTER SIDE OF THE BARGAIN.
OF COURSE THEY'D HAVE TO BE IN THE FAR CORNER OF THE PASTURE — AND ME ABOUT DEAD!
AND NOW WE'LL HAVE TO MILK IN THAT HOT, STUFFY COW BARN.
BOB ARTLEY

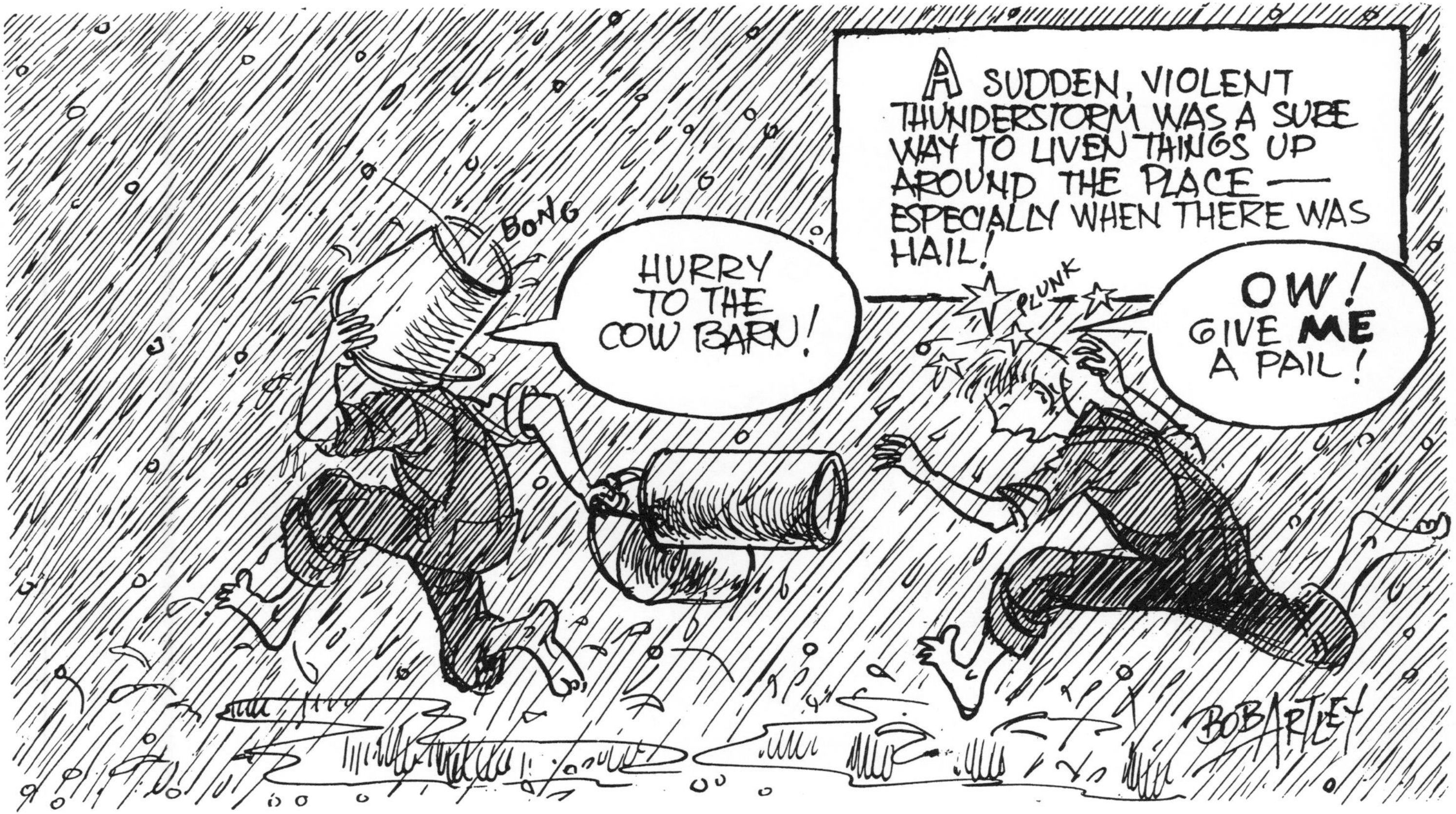
A SUDDEN, VIOLENT THUNDERSTORM WAS A SURE WAY TO LIVEN THINGS UP AROUND THE PLACE— ESPECIALLY WHEN THERE WAS HAIL!
BONG
HURRY TO THE COW BARN!
PLUNK
OW! GIVE ME A PAIL!
BOB ARTLEY

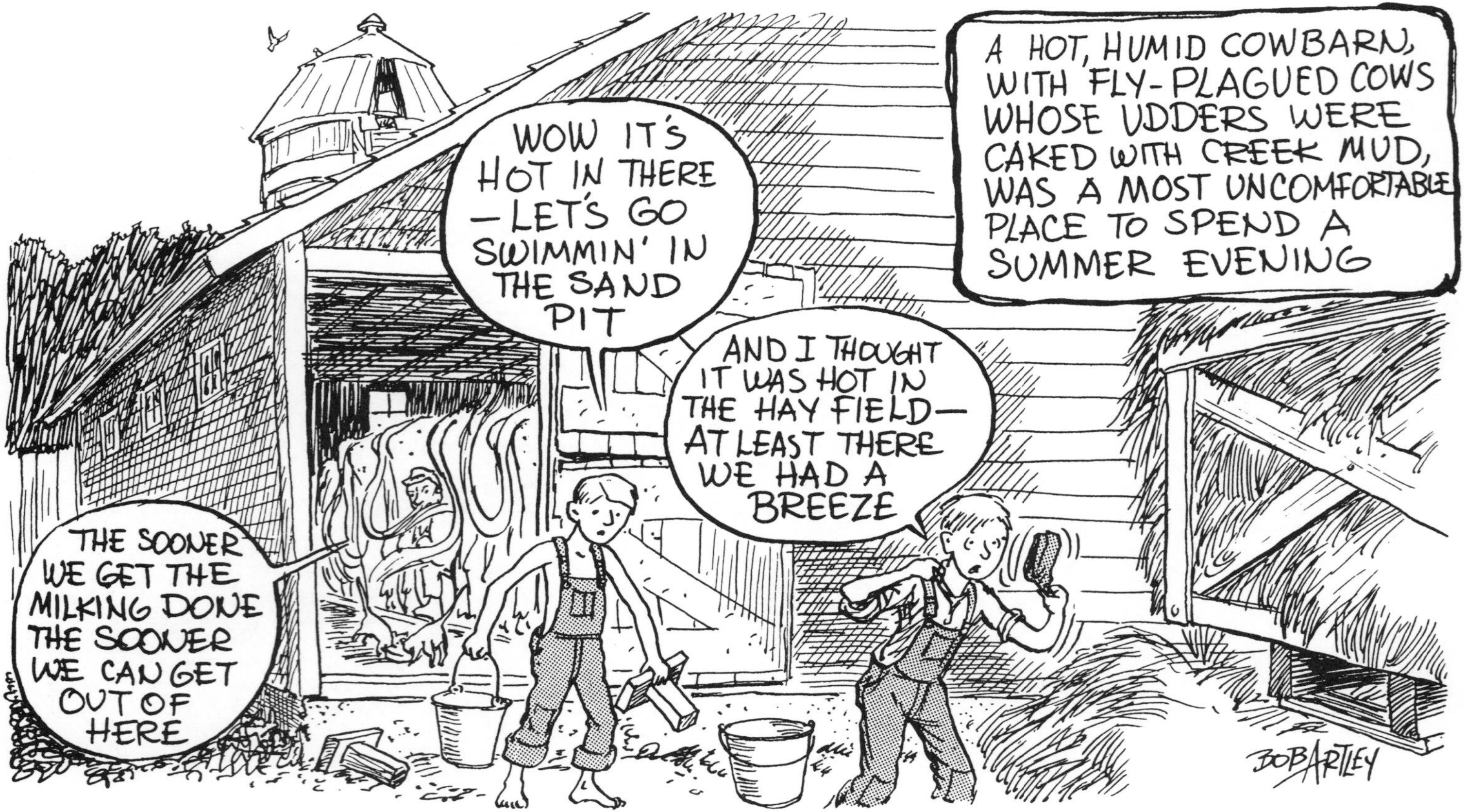
A HOT, HUMID COWBARN, WITH FLY-PLAGUED COWS WHOSE UDDERS WERE CAKED WITH CREEK MUD, WAS A MOST UNCOMFORTABLE PLACE TO SPEND A SUMMER EVENING
WOW IT'S HOT IN THERE —LET'S GO SWIMMIN' IN THE SAND PIT
AND I THOUGHT IT WAS HOT IN THE HAY FIELD— AT LEAST THERE WE HAD A BREEZE
THE SOONER WE GET THE MILKING DONE THE SOONER WE CAN GET OUT OF HERE
BOB ARTLEY

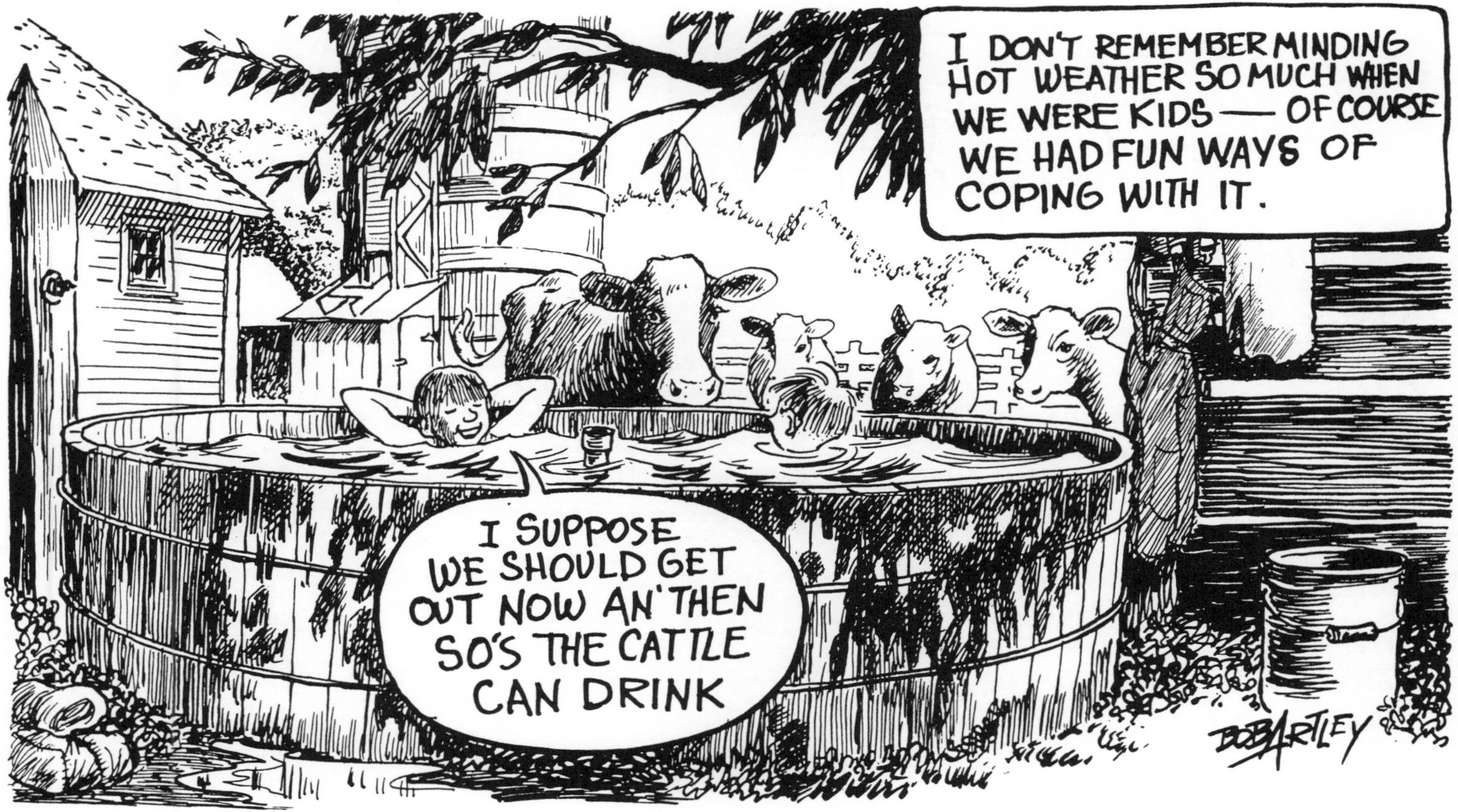
I DON'T REMEMBER MINDING HOT WEATHER SO MUCH WHEN WE WERE KIDS — OF COURSE WE HAD FUN WAYS OF COPING WITH IT.
I SUPPOSE WE SHOULD GET OUT NOW AN' THEN SO'S THE CATTLE CAN DRINK
BOB ARTLEY

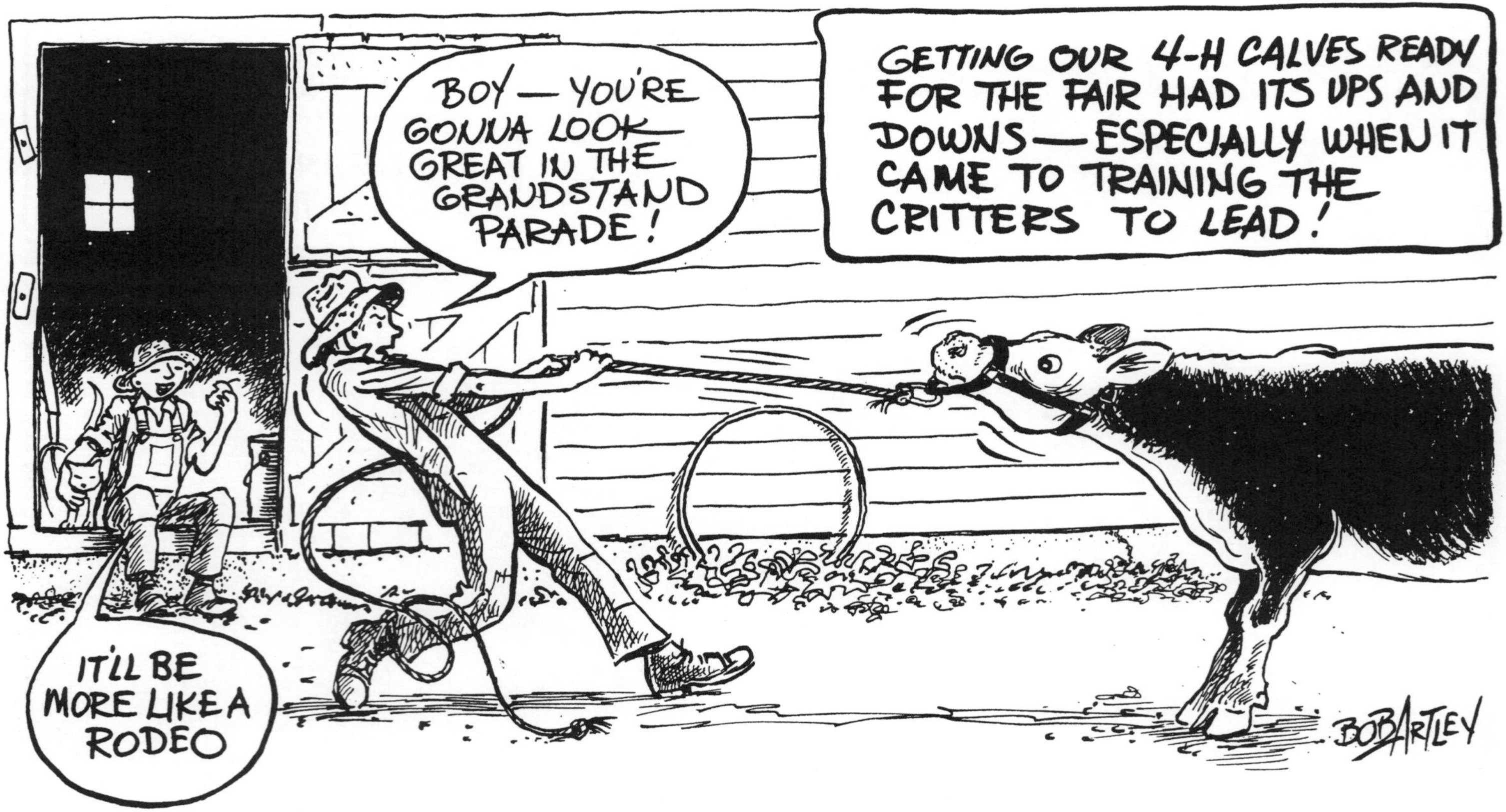
GETTING OUR 4-H CALVES READY FOR THE FAIR HAD ITS UPS AND DOWNS—ESPECIALLY WHEN IT CAME TO TRAINING THE CRITTERS TO LEAD!
BOY—YOU'RE GONNA LOOK GREAT IN THE GRANDSTAND PARADE!
IT'LL BE MORE LIKE A RODEO
BOB ARTLEY

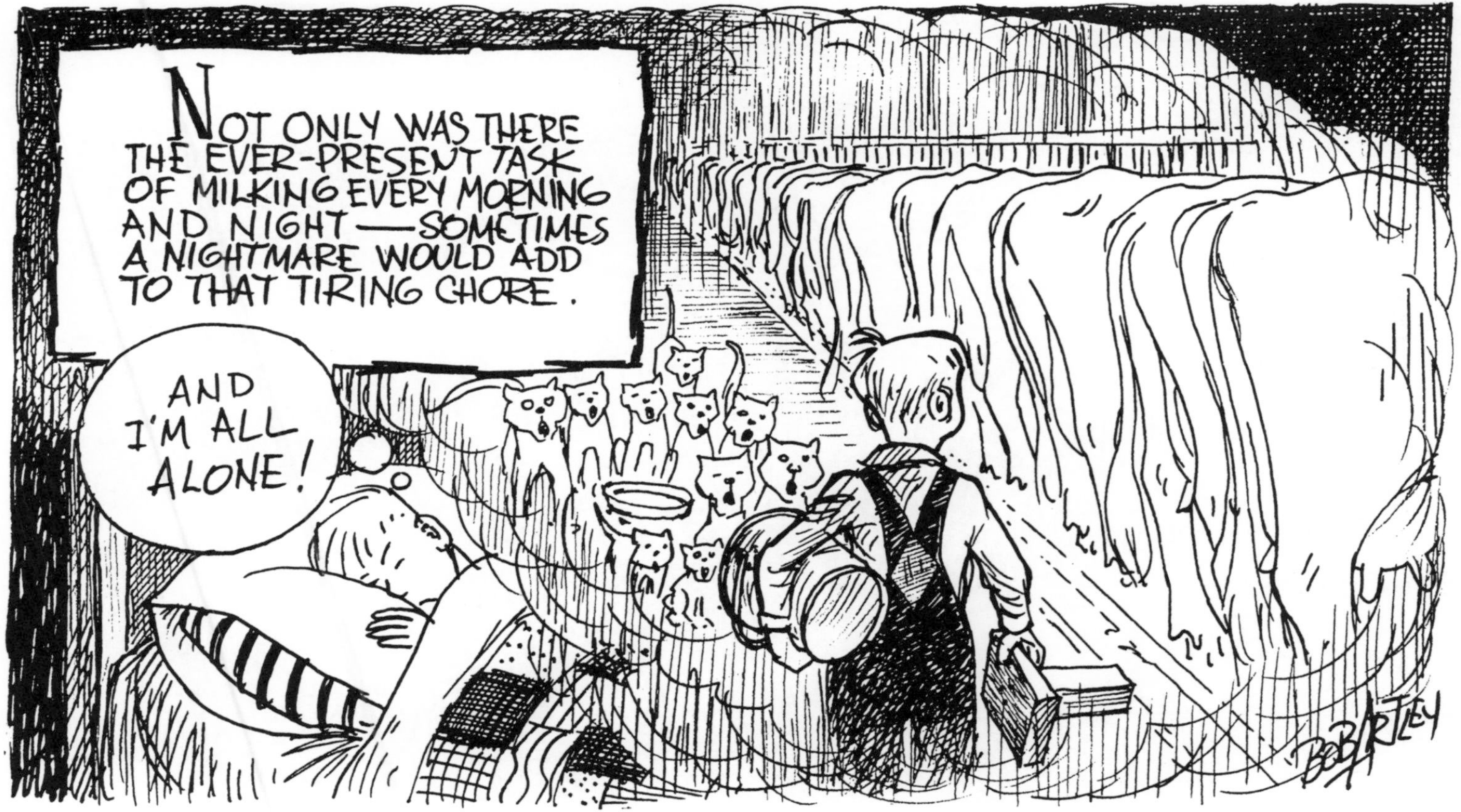
NOT ONLY WAS THERE THE EVER-PRESENT TASK OF MILKING EVERY MORNING AND NIGHT—SOMETIMES A NIGHTMARE WOULD ADD TO THAT TIRING CHORE.
AND I'M ALL ALONE!
BOB ARTLEY

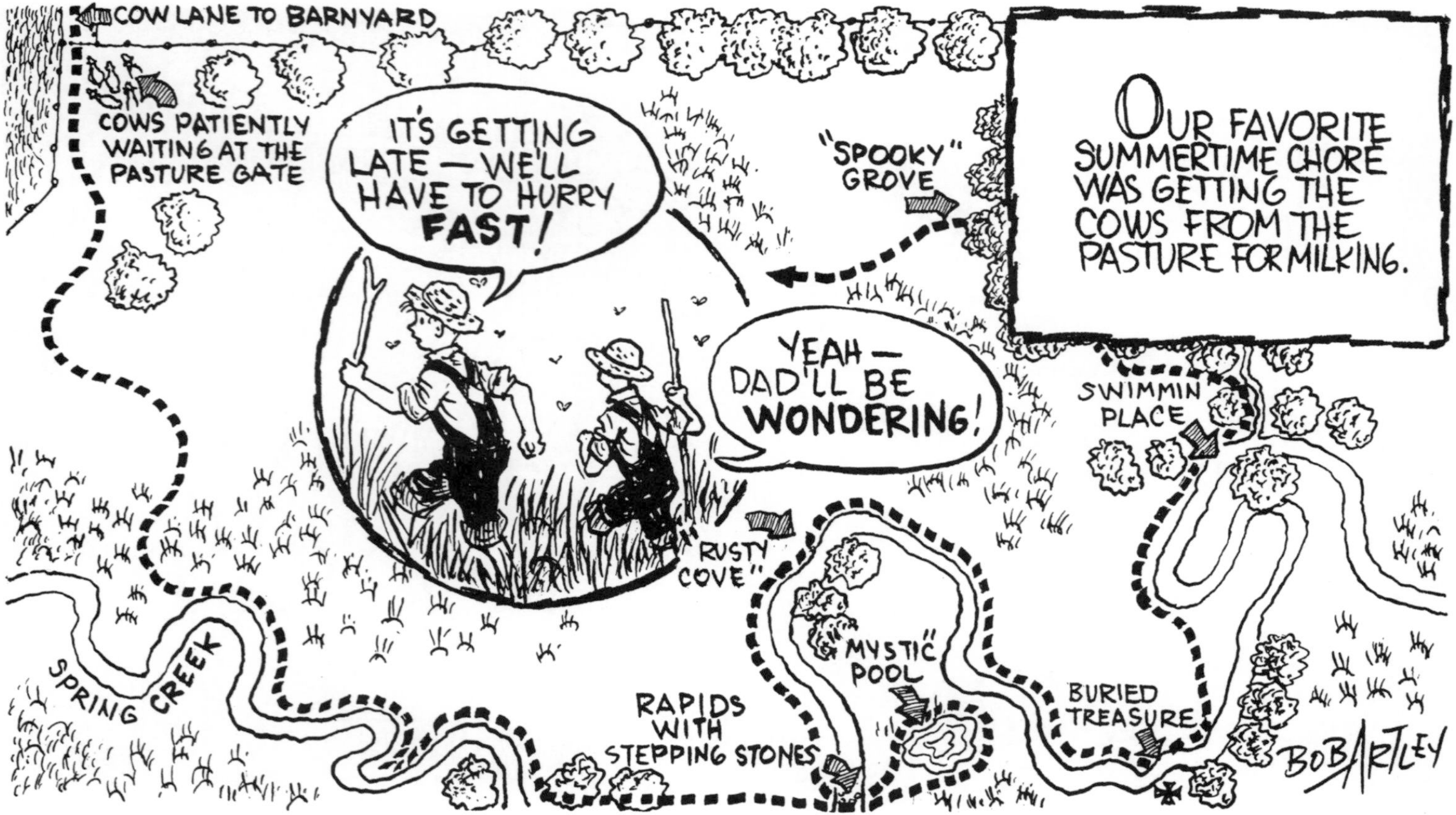

OUR FAVORITE SUMMERTIME CHORE WAS GETTING THE COWS FROM THE PASTURE FOR MILKING.
COW LANE TO BARNYARD
COWS PATIENTLY WAITING AT THE PASTURE GATE
IT'S GETTING LATE — WE'LL HAVE TO HURRY FAST!
YEAH — DAD'LL BE WONDERING!
"SPOOKY" GROVE
SWIMMIN PLACE
"RUSTY COVE"
SPRING CREEK
RAPIDS WITH STEPPING STONES
"MYSTIC" POOL
BURIED TREASURE
BOB ARTLEY

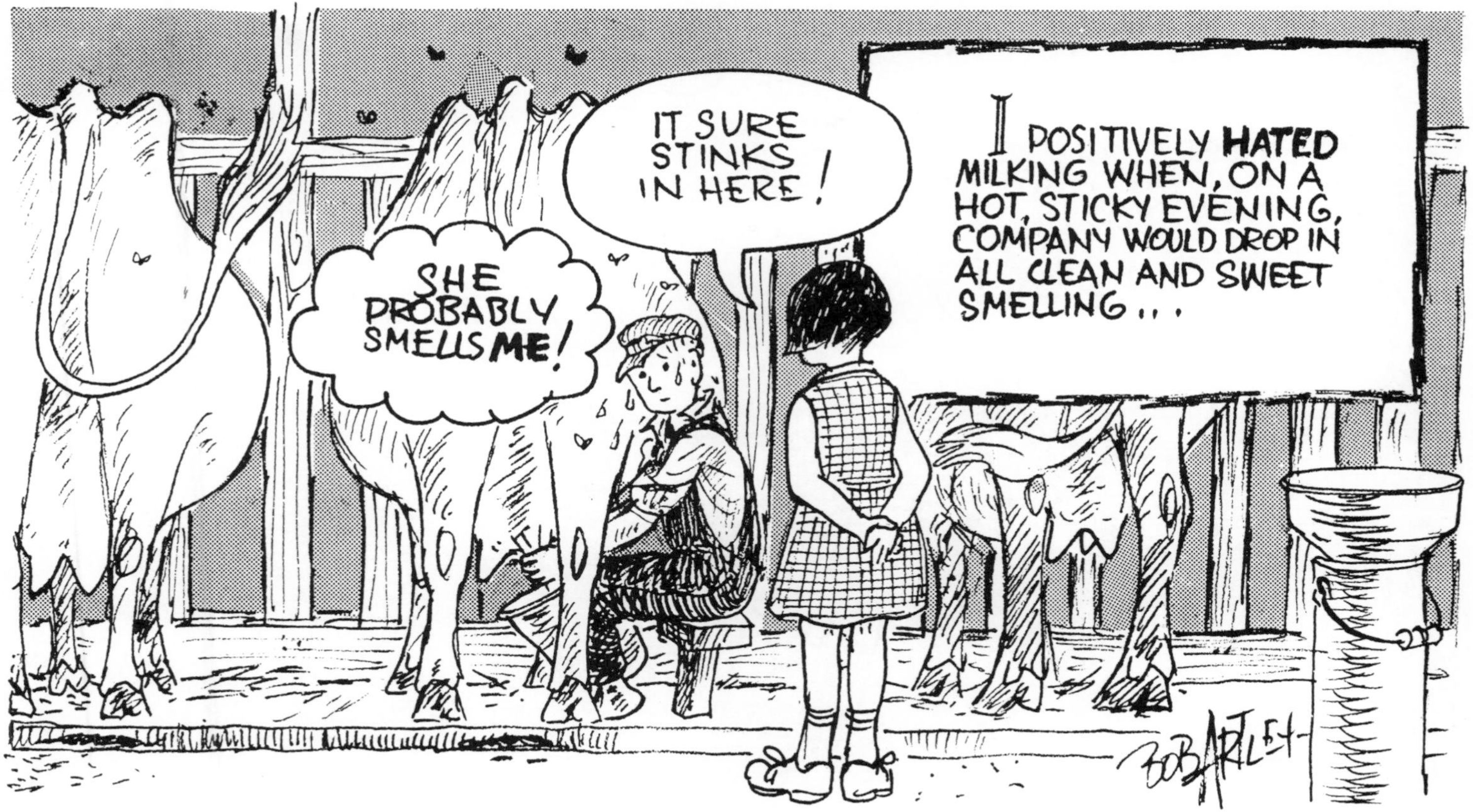
I POSITIVELY **HATED** MILKING WHEN, ON A HOT, STICKY EVENING, COMPANY WOULD DROP IN ALL CLEAN AND SWEET SMELLING . . .
IT SURE STINKS IN HERE!
SHE PROBABLY SMELLS **ME**!
BOB ARTLEY

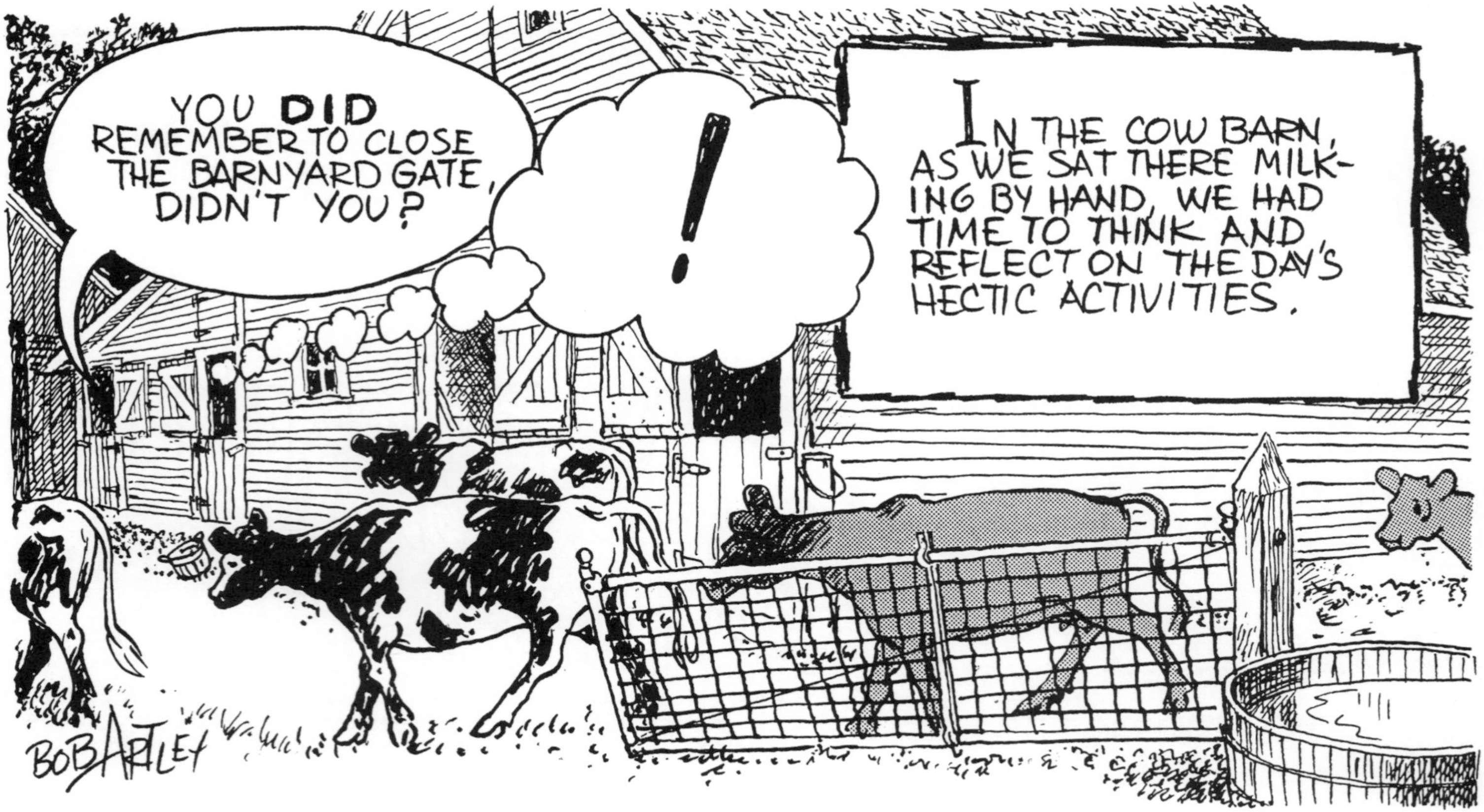
YOU **DID** REMEMBER TO CLOSE THE BARNYARD GATE, DIDN'T YOU?
!
IN THE COW BARN, AS WE SAT THERE MILK-ING BY HAND, WE HAD TIME TO THINK AND REFLECT ON THE DAY'S HECTIC ACTIVITIES.
BOB BARTLEY

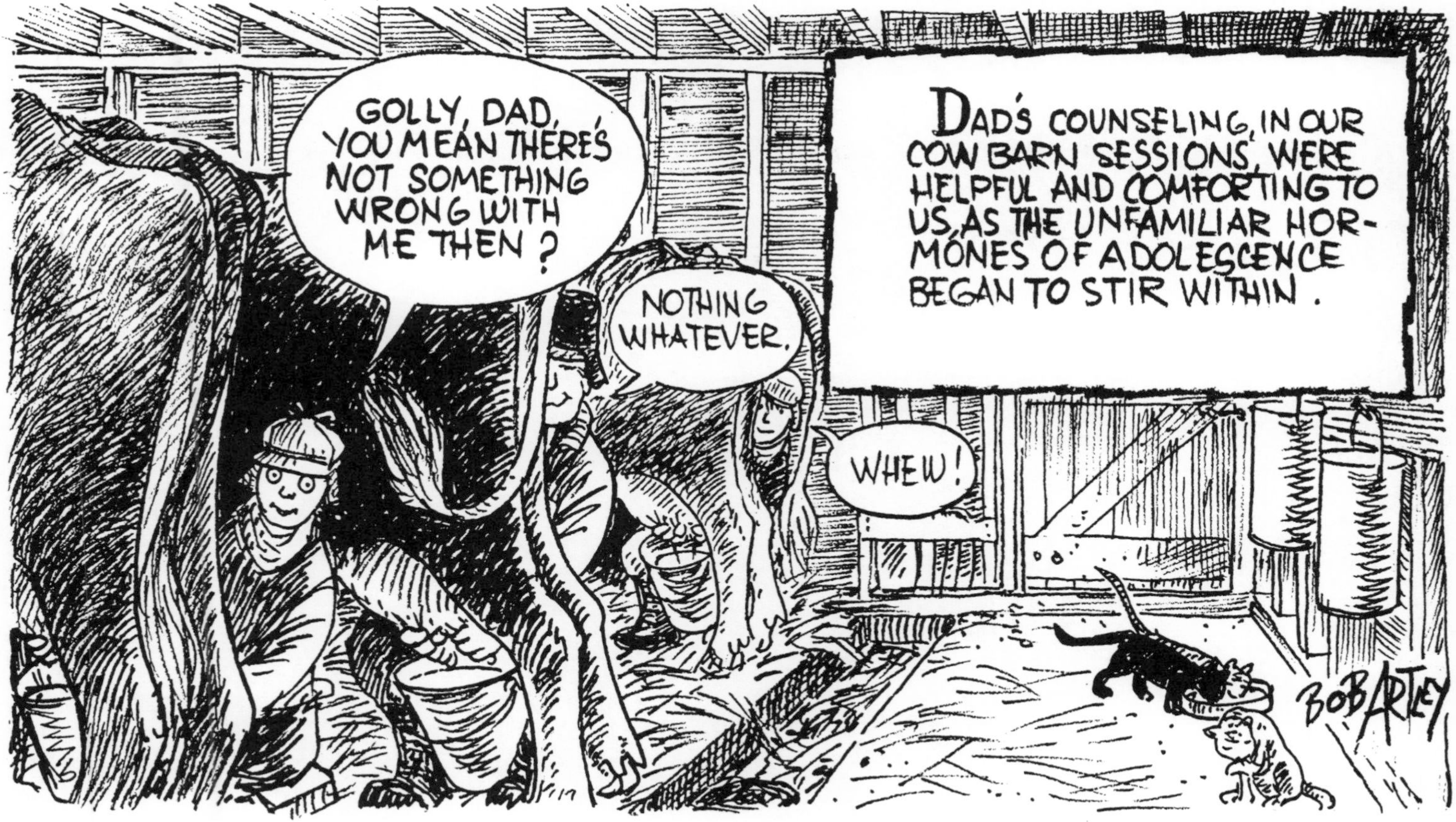
GOLLY, DAD, YOU MEAN THERE'S NOT SOMETHING WRONG WITH ME THEN ?
NOTHING WHATEVER.
WHEW !
DAD'S COUNSELING, IN OUR COW BARN SESSIONS, WERE HELPFUL AND COMFORTING TO US, AS THE UNFAMILIAR HOR-MONES OF ADOLESCENCE BEGAN TO STIR WITHIN.
BOB ARTLEY

Corn

When the scent of green corn announced the presence of ears maturing on the stalks, the cattle seemed to be the first to pick up the message. What had formerly seemed to be a gentle herd of cows grazing contentedly in a peaceful pasture suddenly changed into restless animals with a far-away look in their eyes.

If the pasture bordered on a cornfield, our own or a neighbor's, the fence between had better be a sturdy one, for the cows would patrol up and down the length of it, reaching through for the corn and testing the fence for its weakest place. Up until the invention of the electric fence, mere barbed wire didn't seem to be much of a deterrence in keeping the corn-obsessed cows from plunging right on through to feed on the succulent ears, leaves, and stalks.

Thus it was not unusual during the roasting-ear stage of the corn's development, when going to fetch the cows at milking time, to find the pasture deserted and a section of fence flattened or broken over and evidence of stripped and trodden-down cornstalks at the site.

"The cows are in the corn," was a dreaded alarm call that could shatter the peace of a summer day.

In addition to having to round up the errant critters and get them back into the pasture, it often meant opening another stretch of fence, since they'd forgotten the hole they'd made. The fence then had to be repaired—either replacing broken-off wooden posts or straightening bent-over steel ones.

Invariably at least one of the wayward cows had sustained a wire cut or two. If a teat had been slashed, milking was made more difficult when it was grasped and pulled to extract the milk. The discomfort often caused the cow to respond by a violent kick.

There was hardly a summer that went by that we didn't experience the touchy task of squeezing milk from a very sore teat on a cow that seemed to have forgotten how she got the cut. And by next corn season, if not before, she was eager to get into the corn again.

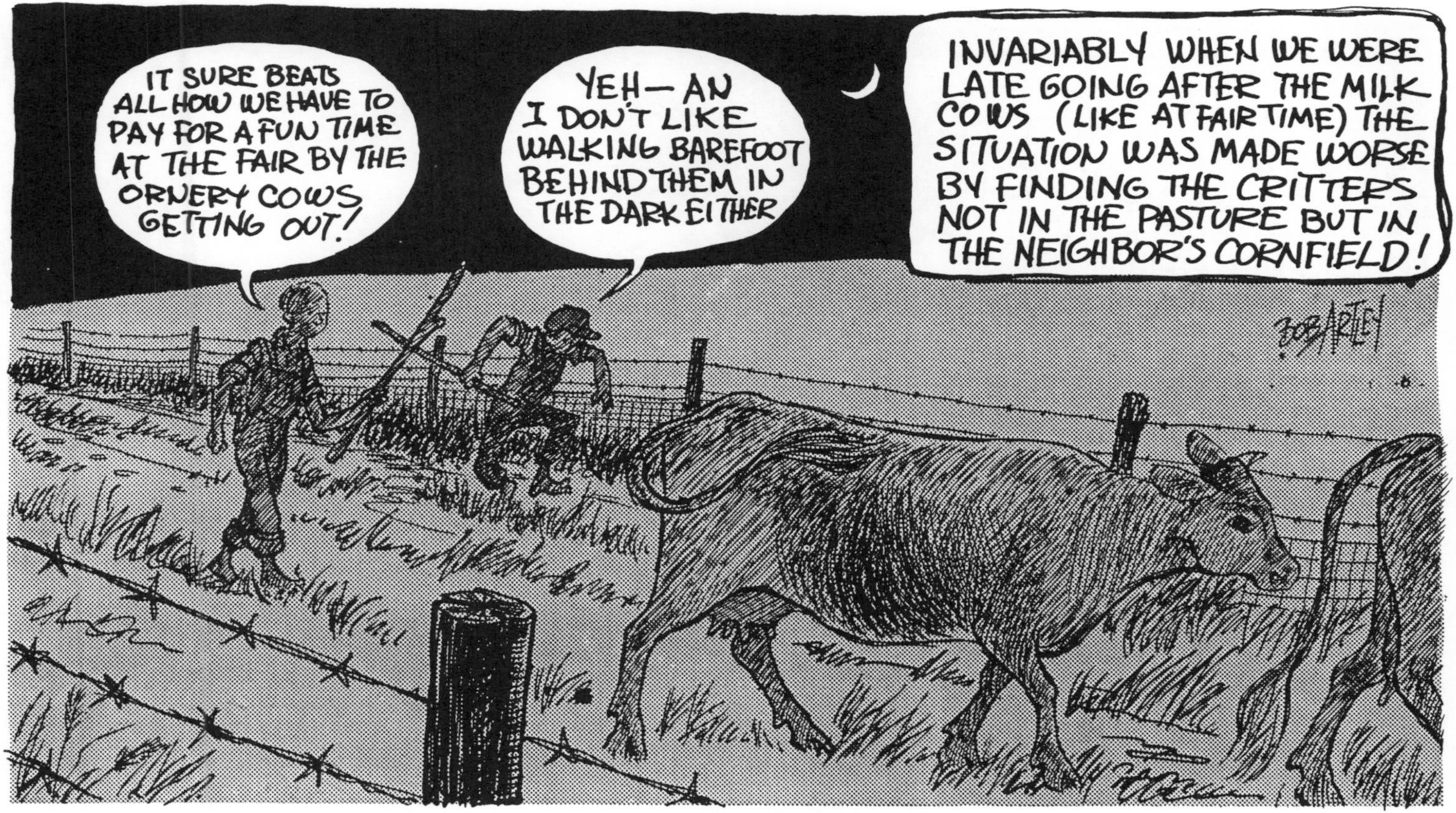
IT SURE BEATS ALL HOW WE HAVE TO PAY FOR A FUN TIME AT THE FAIR BY THE ORNERY COWS GETTING OUT!
YEH— AN I DON'T LIKE WALKING BAREFOOT BEHIND THEM IN THE DARK EITHER
INVARIABLY WHEN WE WERE LATE GOING AFTER THE MILK COWS (LIKE AT FAIR TIME) THE SITUATION WAS MADE WORSE BY FINDING THE CRITTERS NOT IN THE PASTURE BUT IN THE NEIGHBOR'S CORNFIELD!
BOB ARTLEY

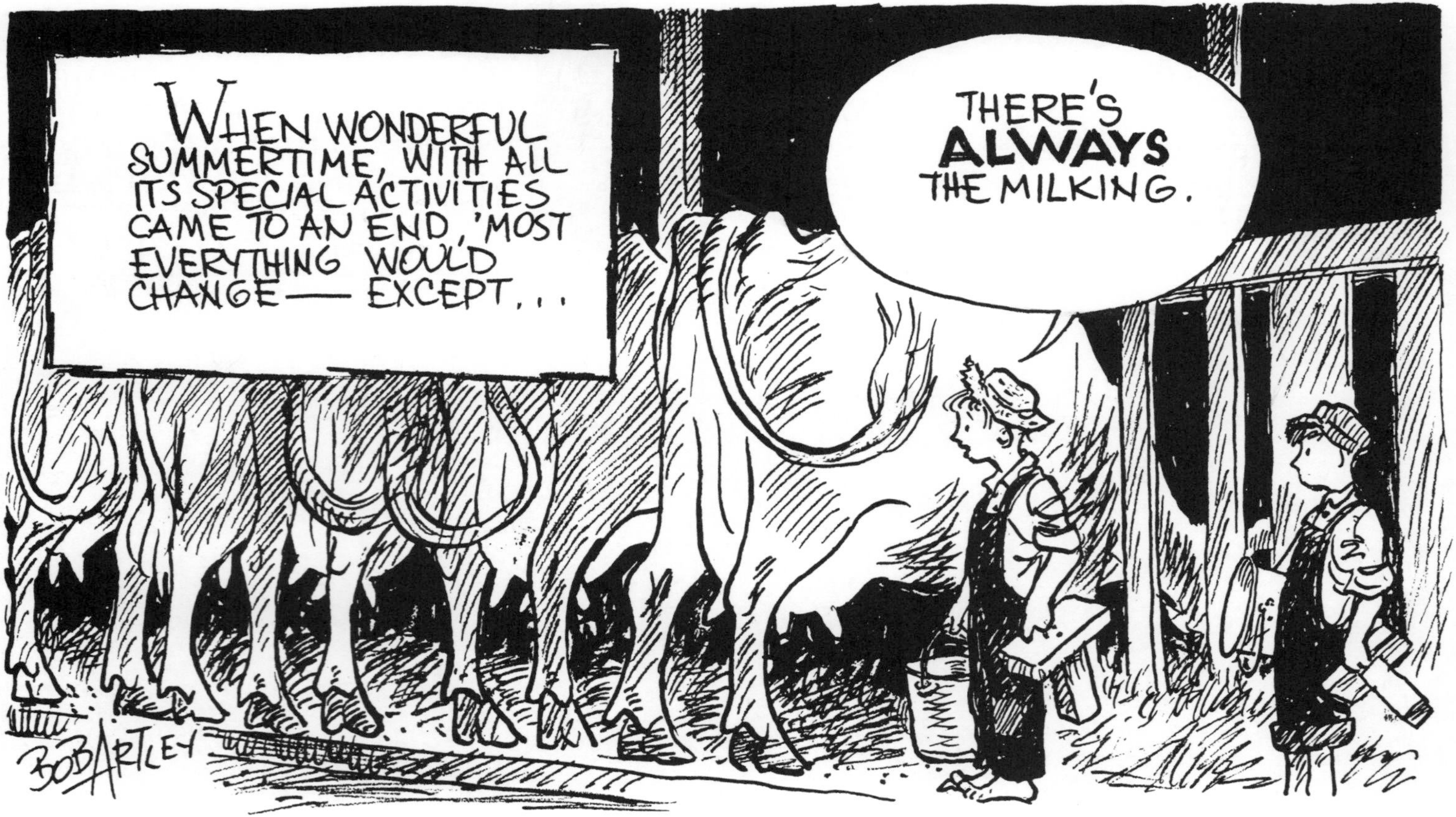
WHEN WONDERFUL SUMMERTIME, WITH ALL ITS SPECIAL ACTIVITIES CAME TO AN END, 'MOST EVERYTHING WOULD CHANGE — EXCEPT...
THERE'S **ALWAYS** THE MILKING.
BOB ARTLEY

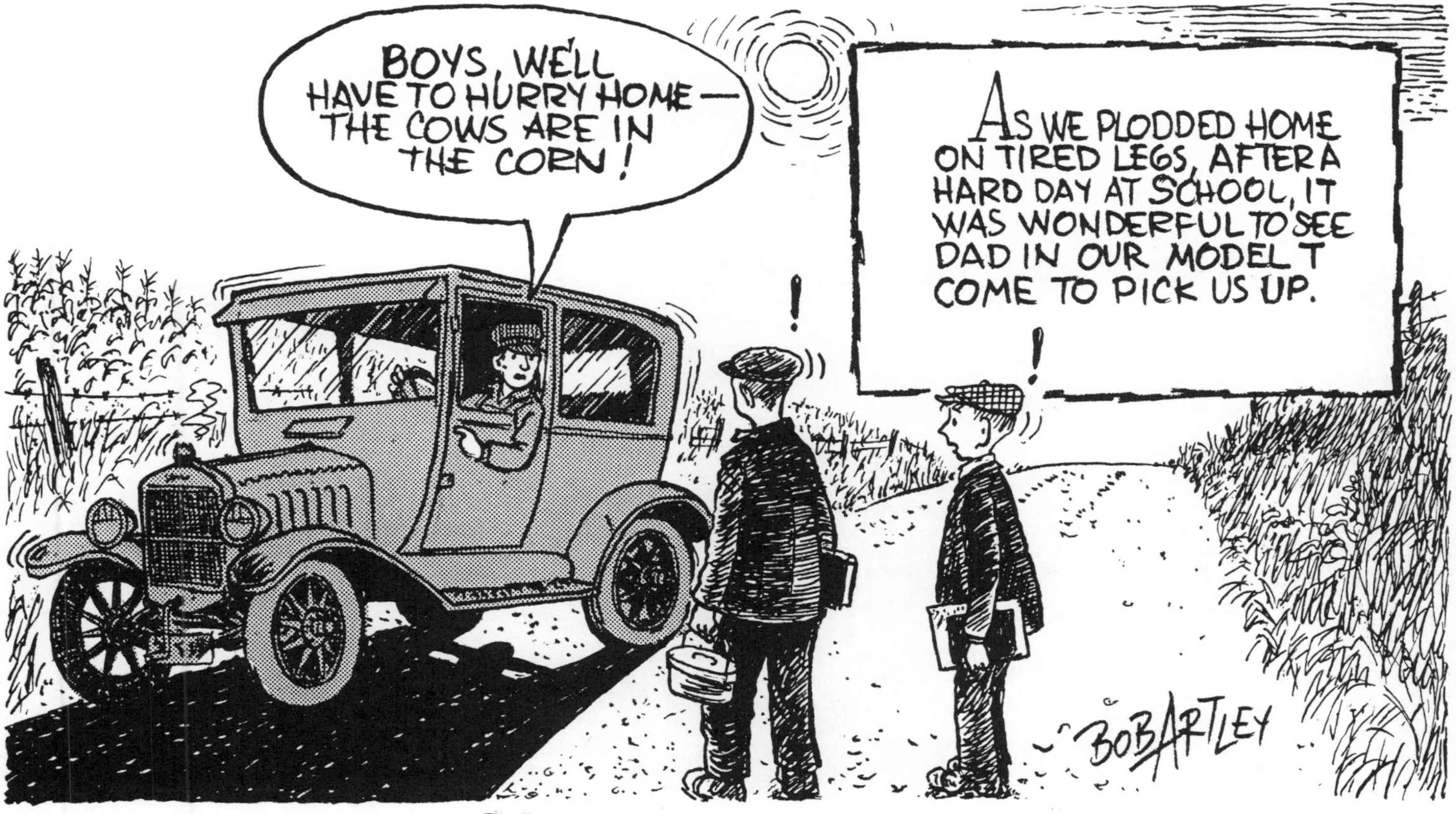
BOYS, WE'LL HAVE TO HURRY HOME— THE COWS ARE IN THE CORN!
AS WE PLODDED HOME ON TIRED LEGS, AFTER A HARD DAY AT SCHOOL, IT WAS WONDERFUL TO SEE DAD IN OUR MODEL T COME TO PICK US UP.
!
!
BOBARTLEY

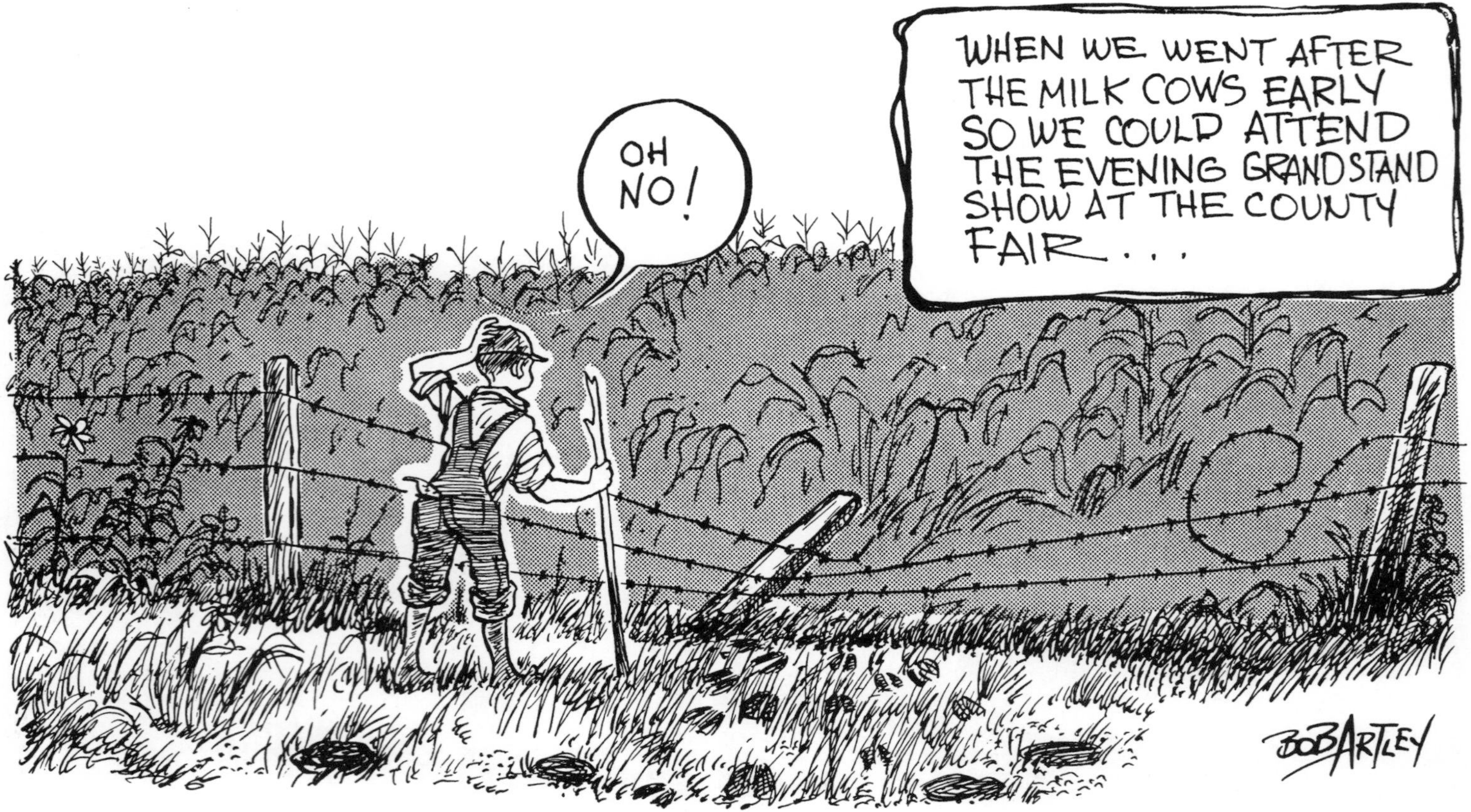
WHEN WE WENT AFTER THE MILK COWS EARLY SO WE COULD ATTEND THE EVENING GRANDSTAND SHOW AT THE COUNTY FAIR . . .
OH NO!
BOB ARTLEY

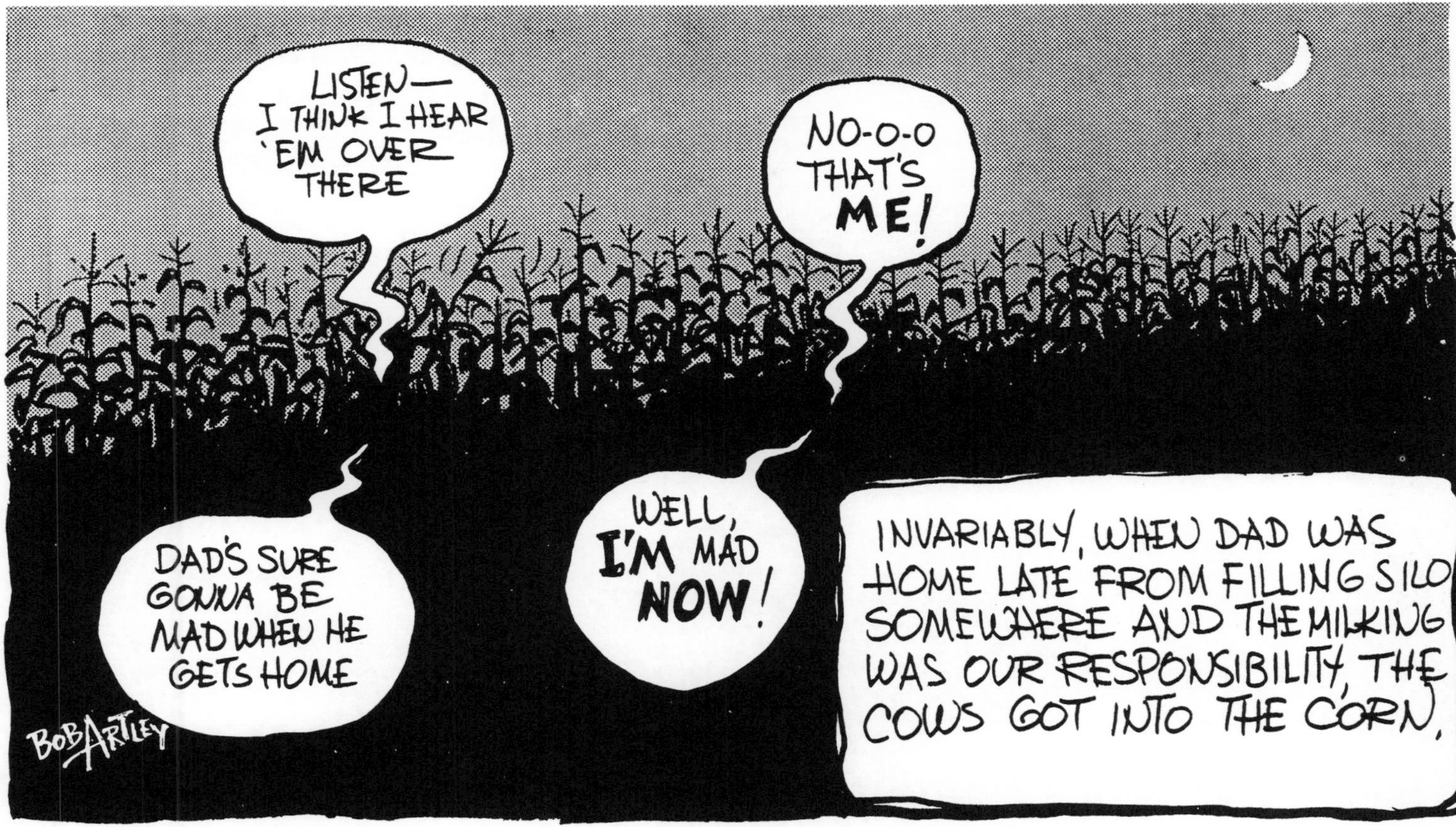
LISTEN—
I THINK I HEAR
'EM OVER
THERE
NO-O-O
THAT'S
ME!
DAD'S SURE
GONNA BE
MAD WHEN HE
GETS HOME
WELL,
I'M MAD
NOW!
INVARIABLY, WHEN DAD WAS HOME LATE FROM FILLING SILO SOMEWHERE AND THE MILKING WAS OUR RESPONSIBILITY, THE COWS GOT INTO THE CORN.
BOB ARTLEY

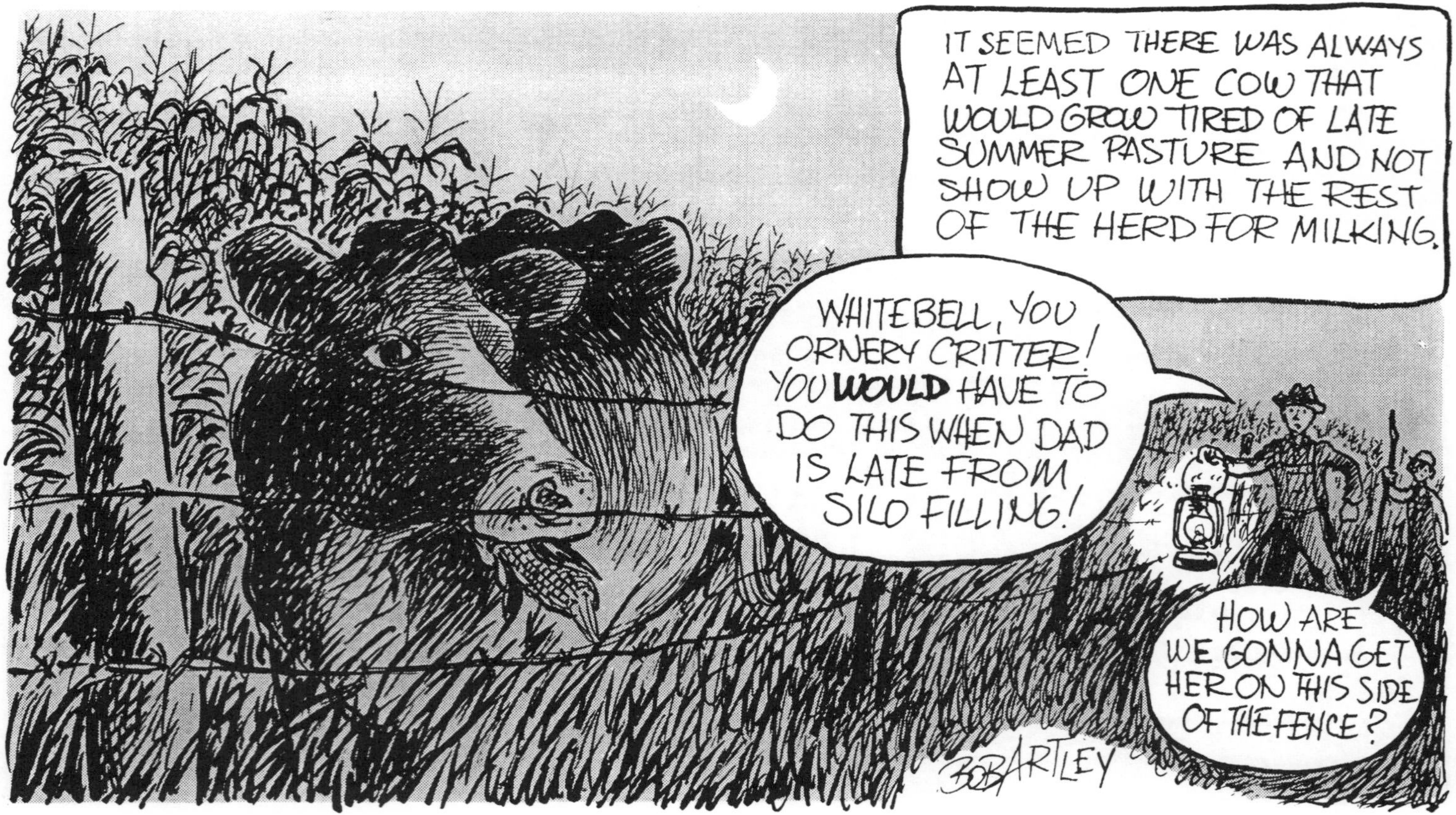
IT SEEMED THERE WAS ALWAYS AT LEAST ONE COW THAT WOULD GROW TIRED OF LATE SUMMER PASTURE AND NOT SHOW UP WITH THE REST OF THE HERD FOR MILKING.
WHITEBELL, YOU ORNERY CRITTER! YOU **WOULD** HAVE TO DO THIS WHEN DAD IS LATE FROM SILO FILLING!
HOW ARE WE GONNA GET HER ON THIS SIDE OF THE FENCE?
BOB ARTLEY

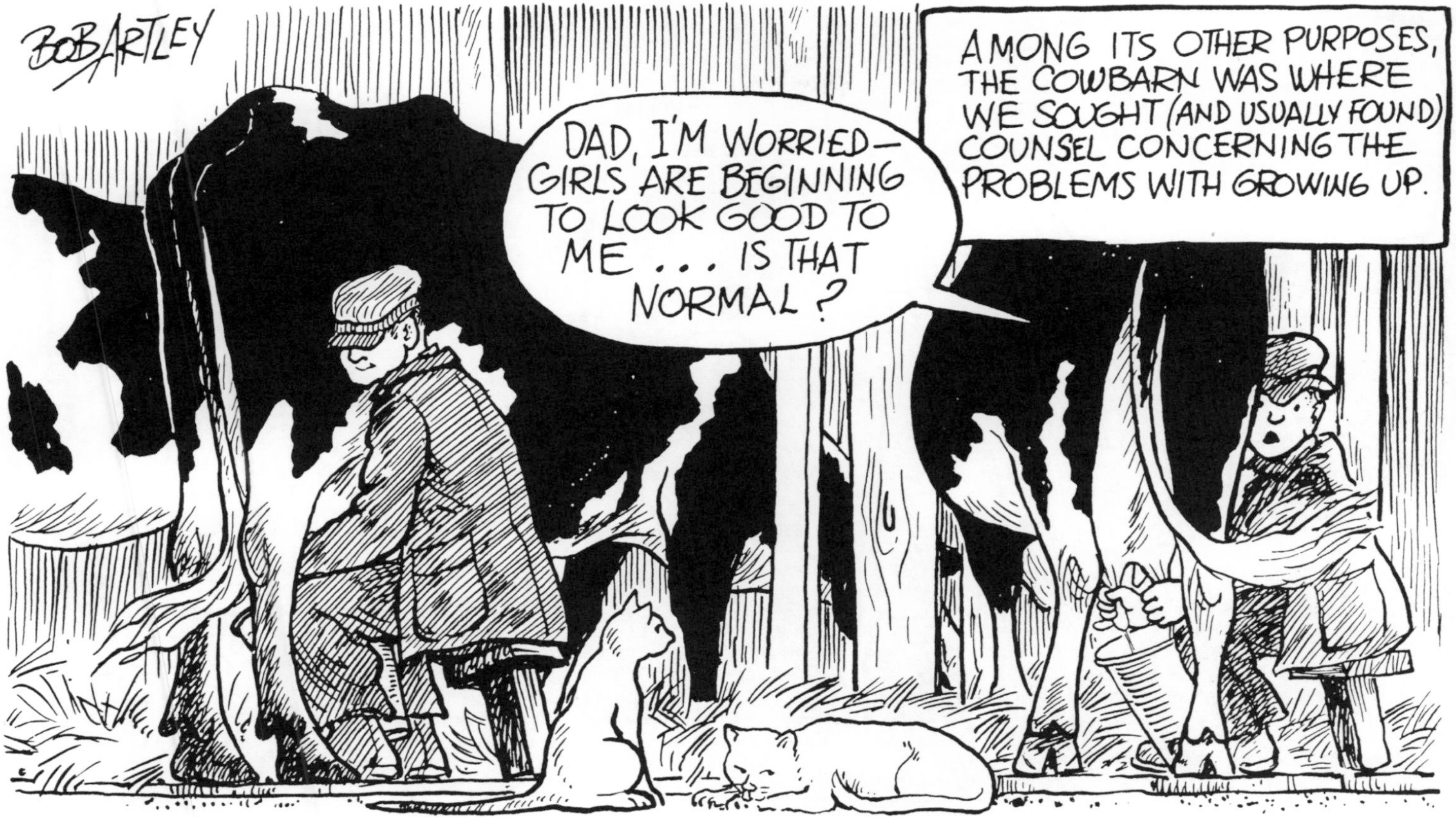
BOB ARTLEY
AMONG ITS OTHER PURPOSES, THE COWBARN WAS WHERE WE SOUGHT (AND USUALLY FOUND) COUNSEL CONCERNING THE PROBLEMS WITH GROWING UP.
DAD, I'M WORRIED— GIRLS ARE BEGINNING TO LOOK GOOD TO ME . . . IS THAT NORMAL ?

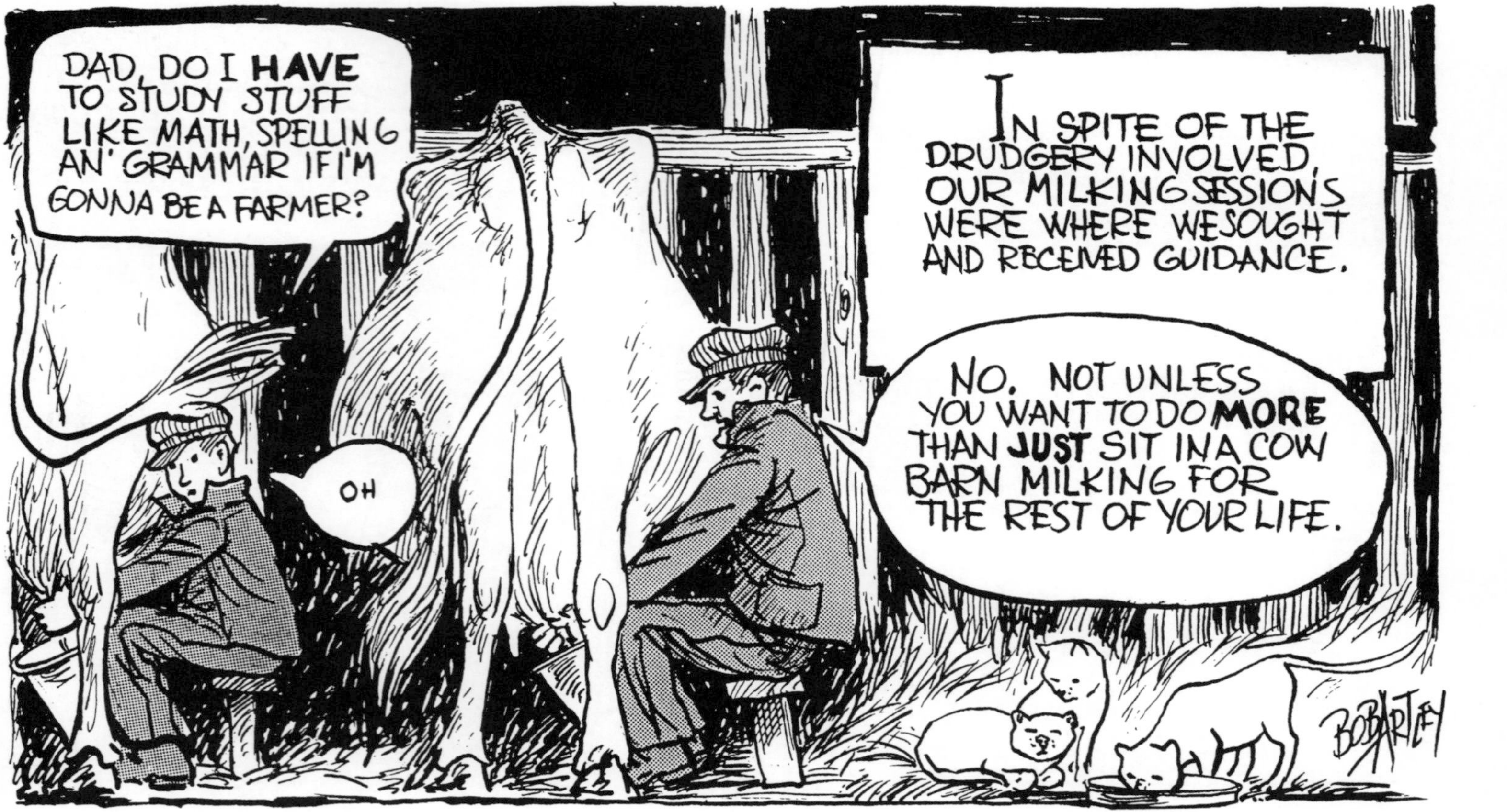
DAD, DO I HAVE TO STUDY STUFF LIKE MATH, SPELLING AN' GRAMMAR IF I'M GONNA BE A FARMER?
IN SPITE OF THE DRUDGERY INVOLVED, OUR MILKING SESSIONS WERE WHERE WE SOUGHT AND RECEIVED GUIDANCE.
NO. NOT UNLESS YOU WANT TO DO MORE THAN JUST SIT IN A COW BARN MILKING FOR THE REST OF YOUR LIFE.
OH
BOB ARTLEY

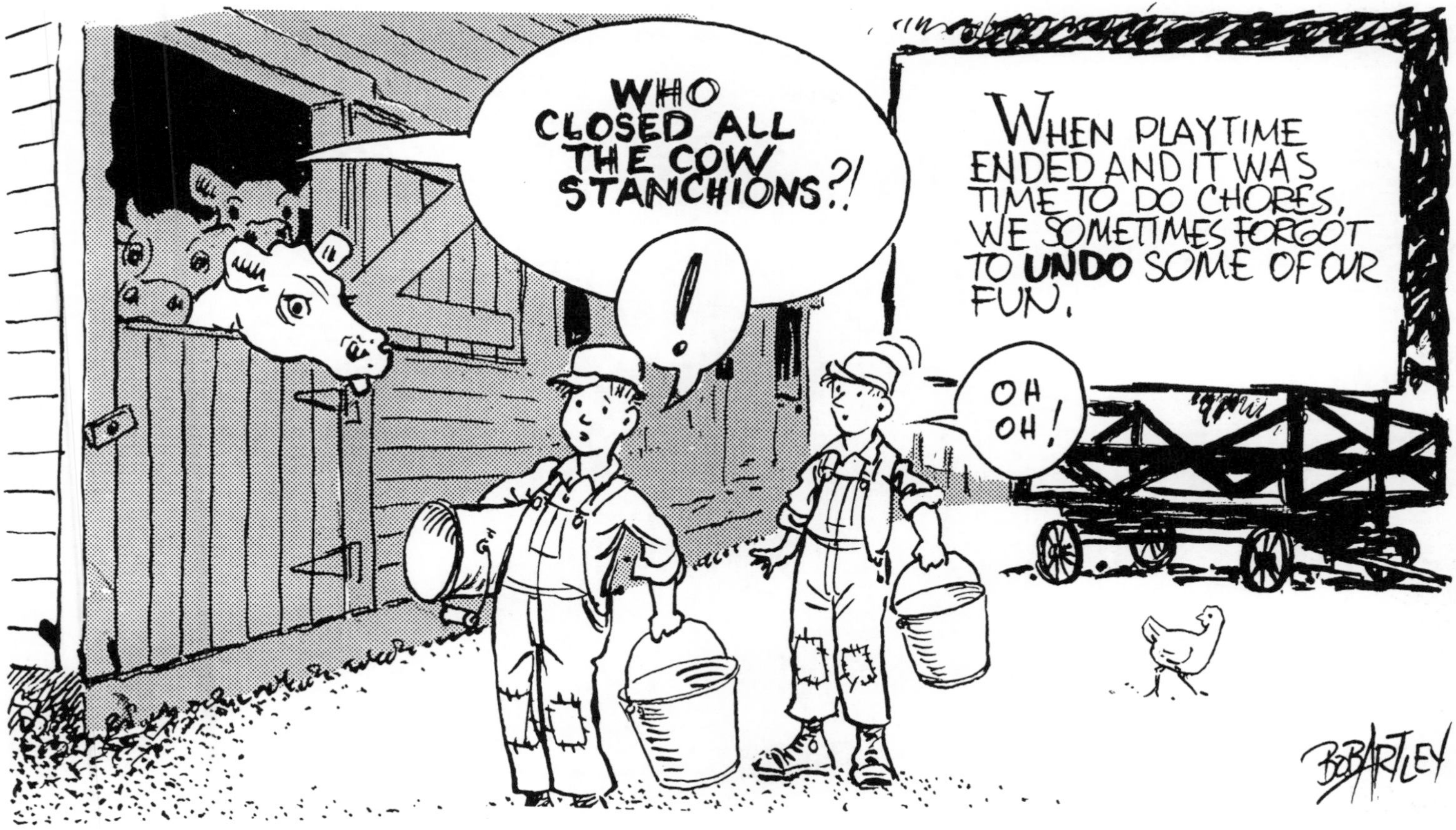
WHO CLOSED ALL THE COW STANCHIONS?!
!
OH OH!
WHEN PLAYTIME ENDED AND IT WAS TIME TO DO CHORES, WE SOMETIMES FORGOT TO **UNDO** SOME OF OUR FUN.
BOBARTLEY

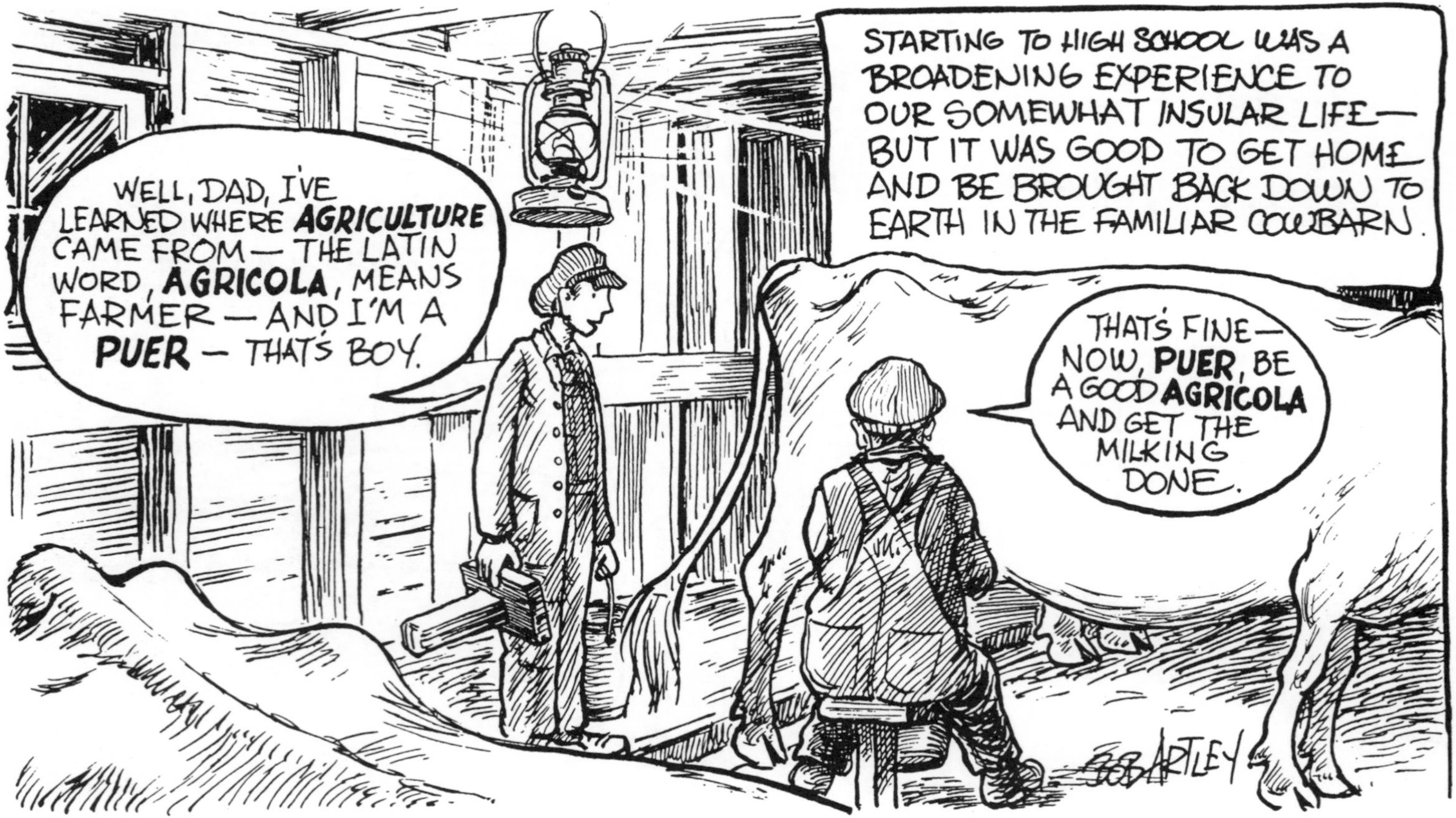
STARTING TO HIGH SCHOOL WAS A BROADENING EXPERIENCE TO OUR SOMEWHAT INSULAR LIFE— BUT IT WAS GOOD TO GET HOME AND BE BROUGHT BACK DOWN TO EARTH IN THE FAMILIAR COWBARN.
WELL, DAD, I'VE LEARNED WHERE **AGRICULTURE** CAME FROM— THE LATIN WORD, **AGRICOLA**, MEANS FARMER—AND I'M A **PUER**—THAT'S BOY.
THAT'S FINE— NOW, **PUER**, BE A GOOD **AGRICOLA** AND GET THE MILKING DONE.
BOB ARTLEY

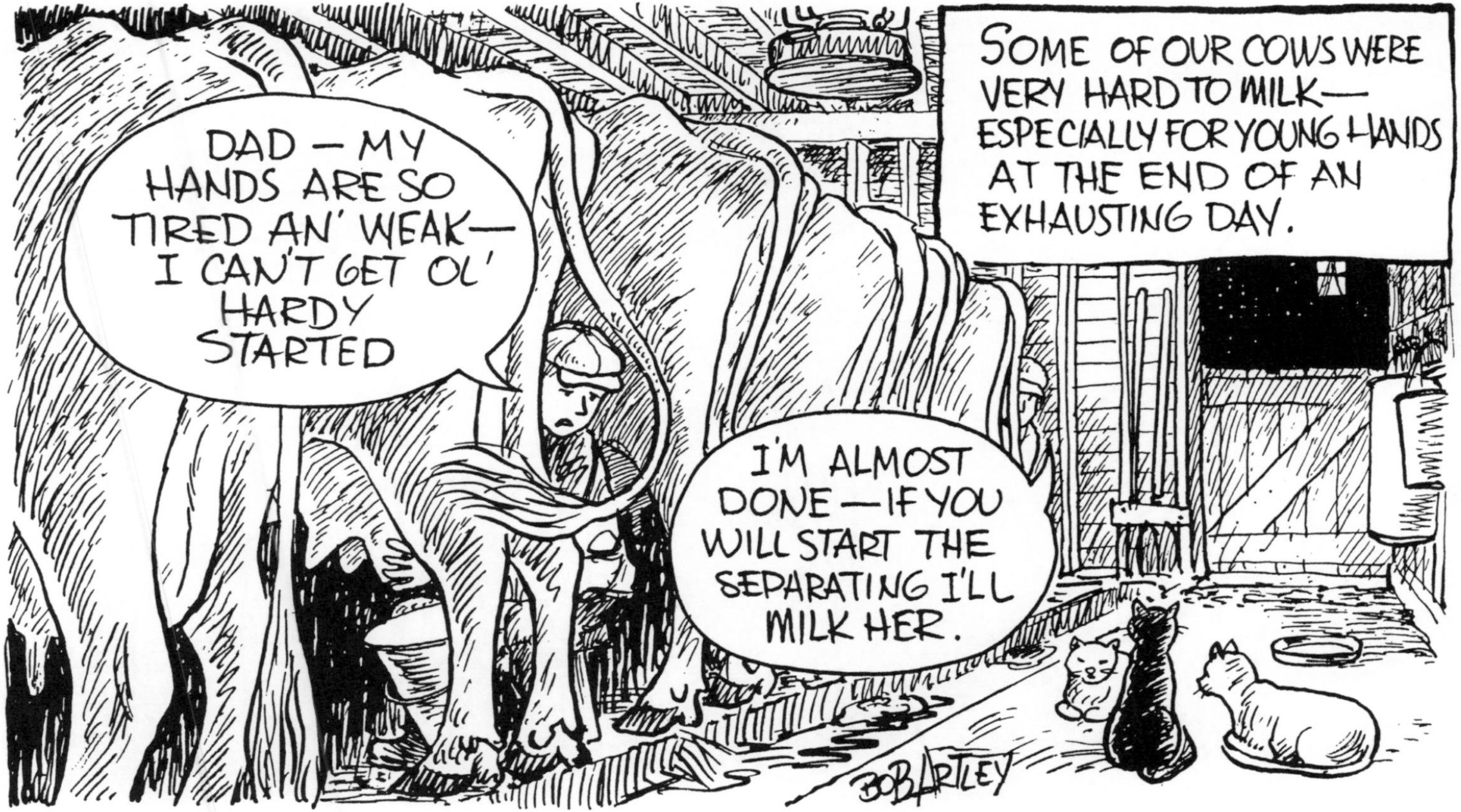
SOME OF OUR COWS WERE VERY HARD TO MILK— ESPECIALLY FOR YOUNG HANDS AT THE END OF AN EXHAUSTING DAY.
DAD — MY HANDS ARE SO TIRED AN' WEAK— I CAN'T GET OL' HARDY STARTED
I'M ALMOST DONE — IF YOU WILL START THE SEPARATING I'LL MILK HER.
BOB ARTLEY

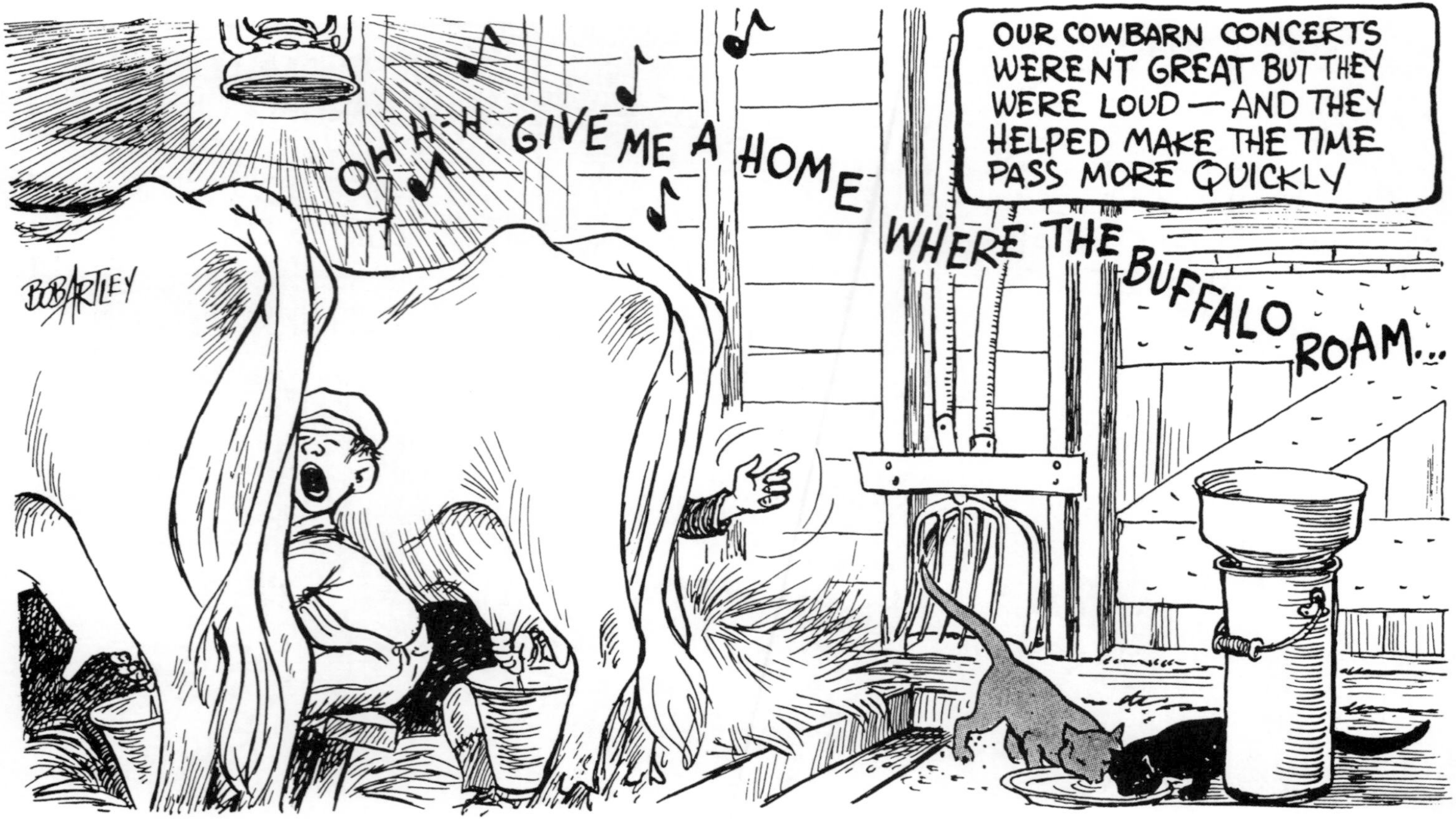
OUR COWBARN CONCERTS WEREN'T GREAT BUT THEY WERE LOUD — AND THEY HELPED MAKE THE TIME PASS MORE QUICKLY
OH-H-H GIVE ME A HOME
WHERE THE BUFFALO ROAM...
BOB ARTLEY

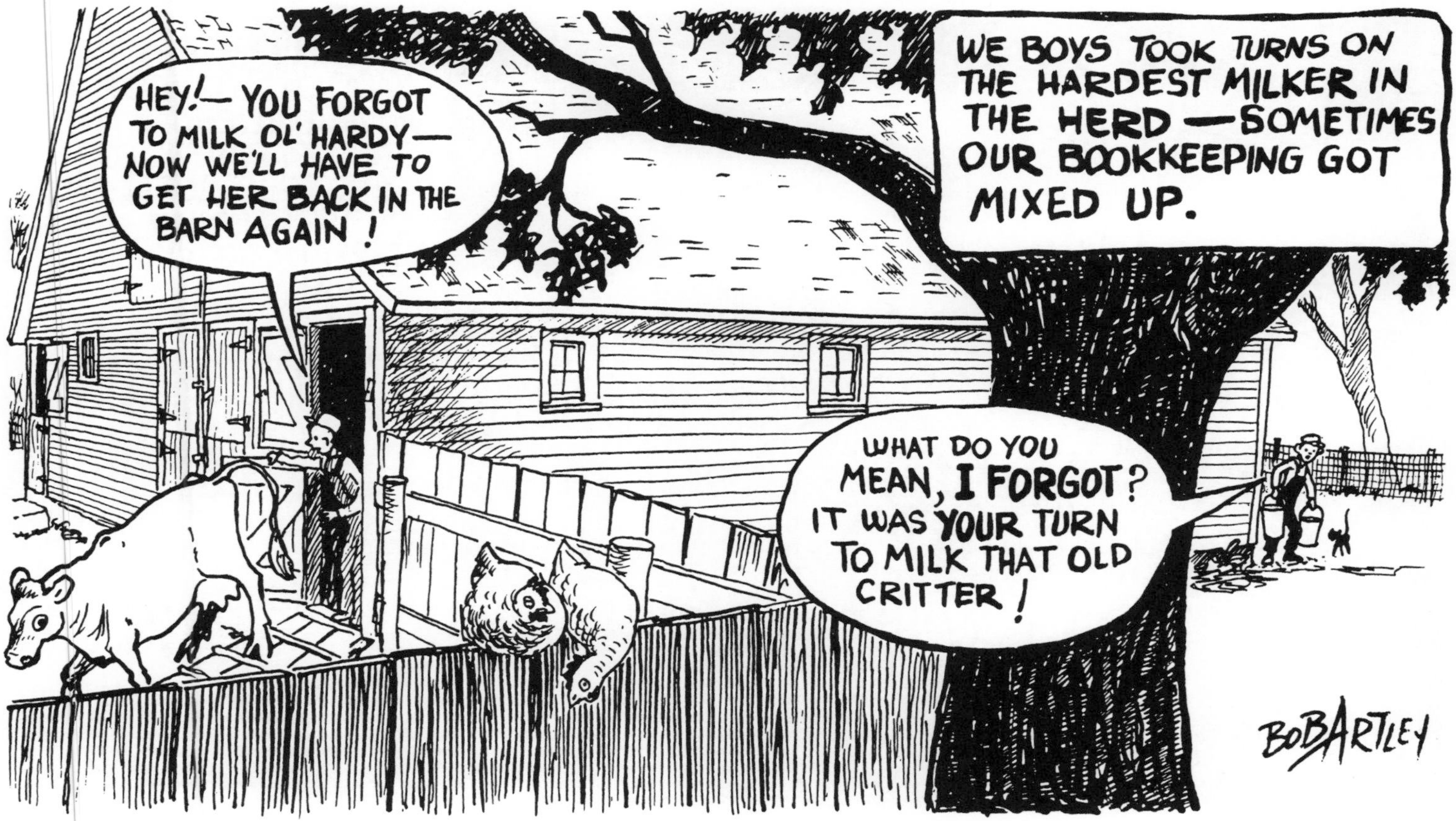
WE BOYS TOOK TURNS ON THE HARDEST MILKER IN THE HERD — SOMETIMES OUR BOOKKEEPING GOT MIXED UP.
HEY! — YOU FORGOT TO MILK OL' HARDY — NOW WE'LL HAVE TO GET HER BACK IN THE BARN AGAIN!
WHAT DO YOU MEAN, I FORGOT? IT WAS YOUR TURN TO MILK THAT OLD CRITTER!
BOBARTLEY

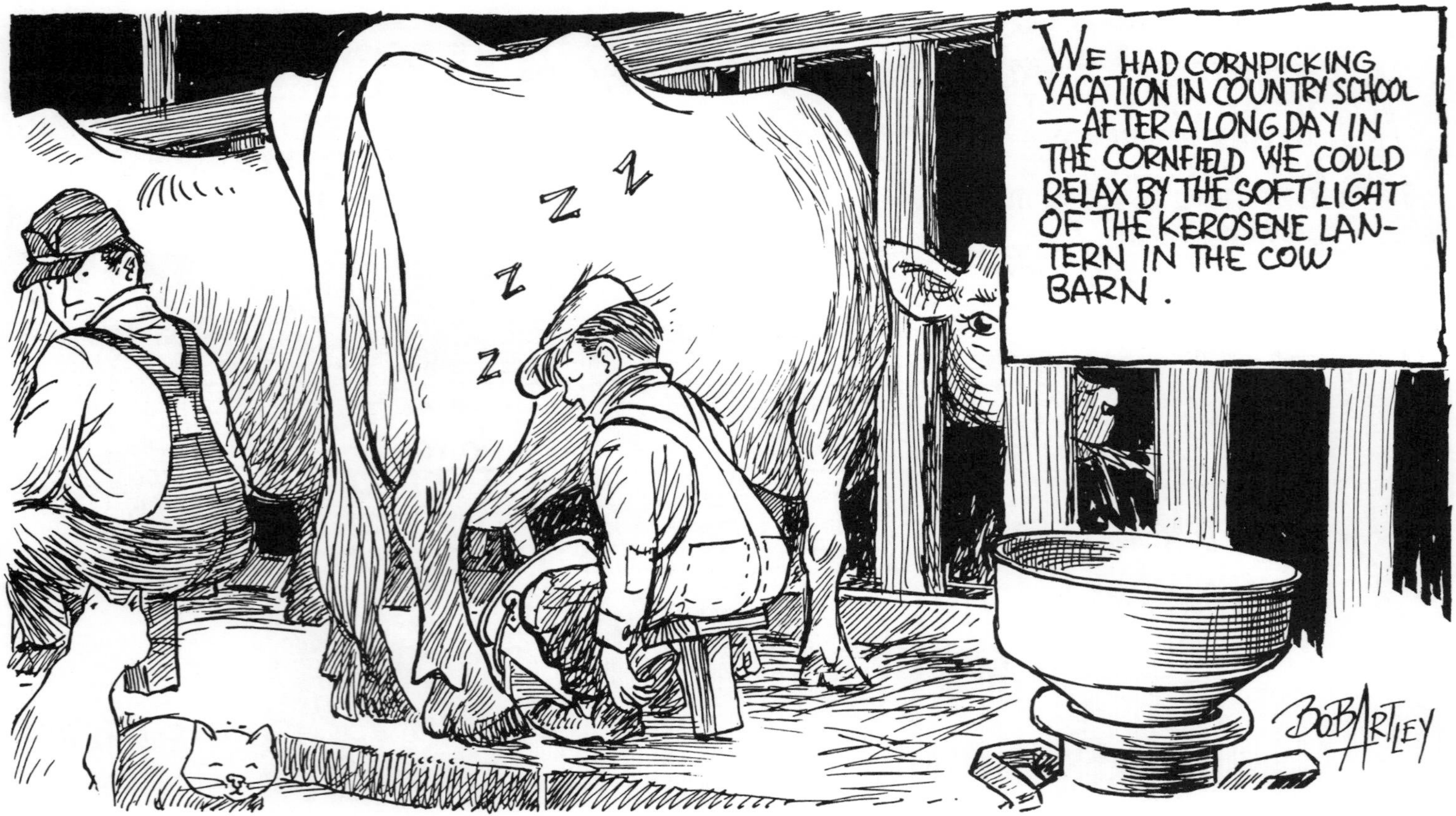
WE HAD CORNPICKING
VACATION IN COUNTRY SCHOOL
—AFTER A LONG DAY IN
THE CORNFIELD WE COULD
RELAX BY THE SOFT LIGHT
OF THE KEROSENE LAN-
TERN IN THE COW
BARN.
Z Z Z Z Z
BOB ARTLEY

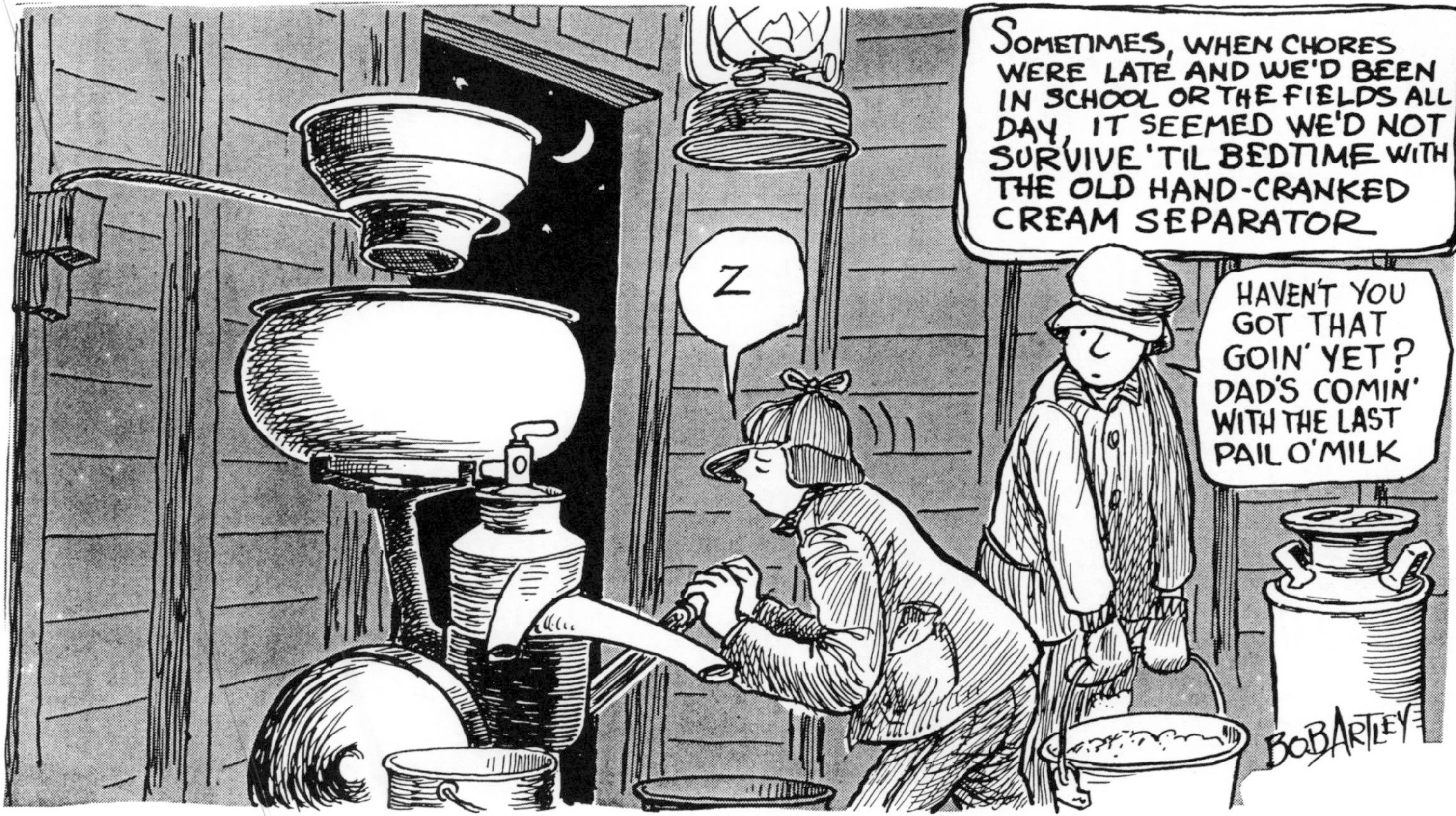
SOMETIMES, WHEN CHORES WERE LATE AND WE'D BEEN IN SCHOOL OR THE FIELDS ALL DAY, IT SEEMED WE'D NOT SURVIVE 'TIL BEDTIME WITH THE OLD HAND-CRANKED CREAM SEPARATOR
Z
HAVEN'T YOU GOT THAT GOIN' YET? DAD'S COMIN' WITH THE LAST PAIL O'MILK
BOB ARTLEY

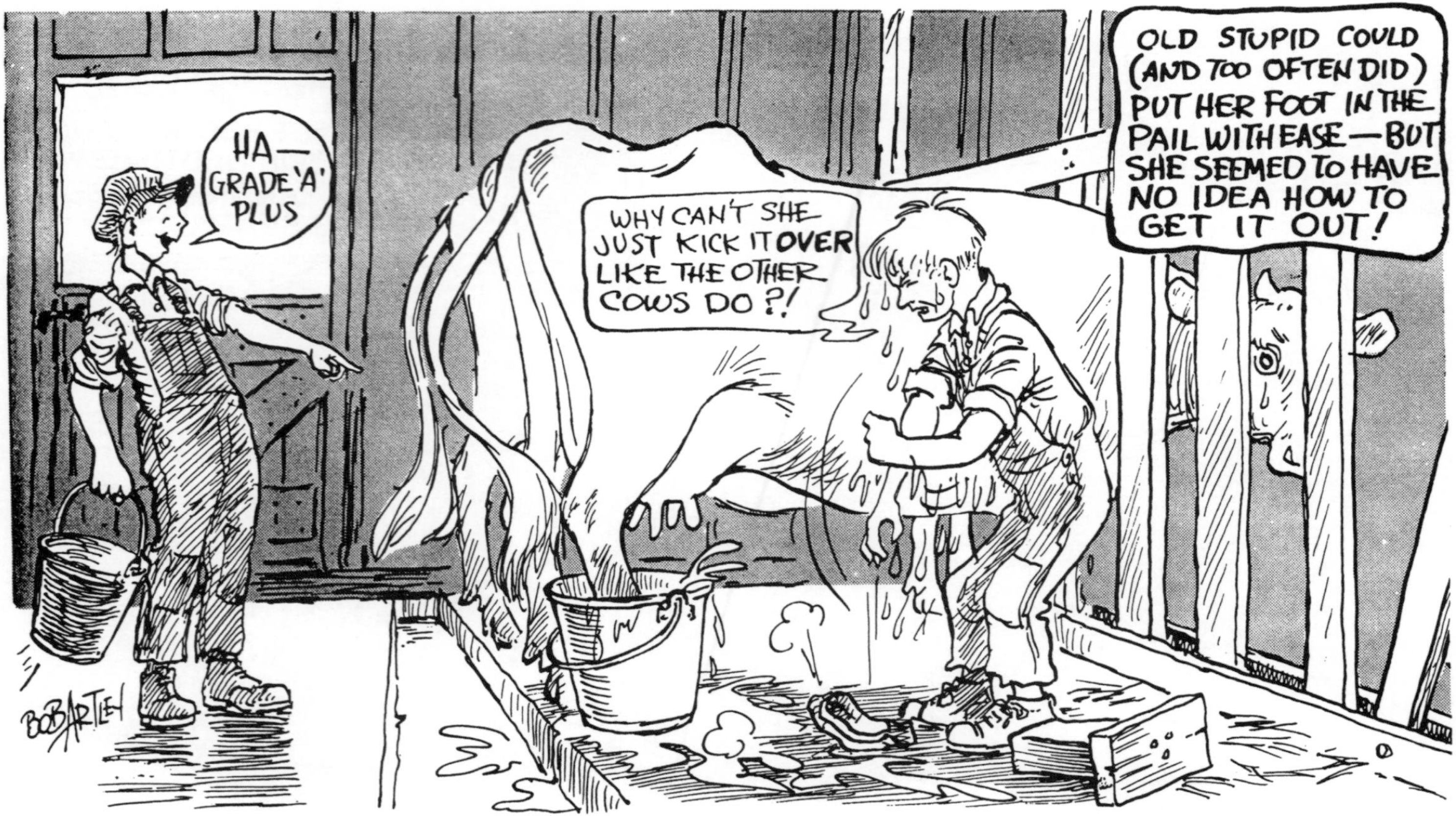
HA— GRADE 'A' PLUS
WHY CAN'T SHE JUST KICK IT OVER LIKE THE OTHER COWS DO?!
OLD STUPID COULD (AND TOO OFTEN DID) PUT HER FOOT IN THE PAIL WITH EASE—BUT SHE SEEMED TO HAVE NO IDEA HOW TO GET IT OUT!
BOB ARTLEY

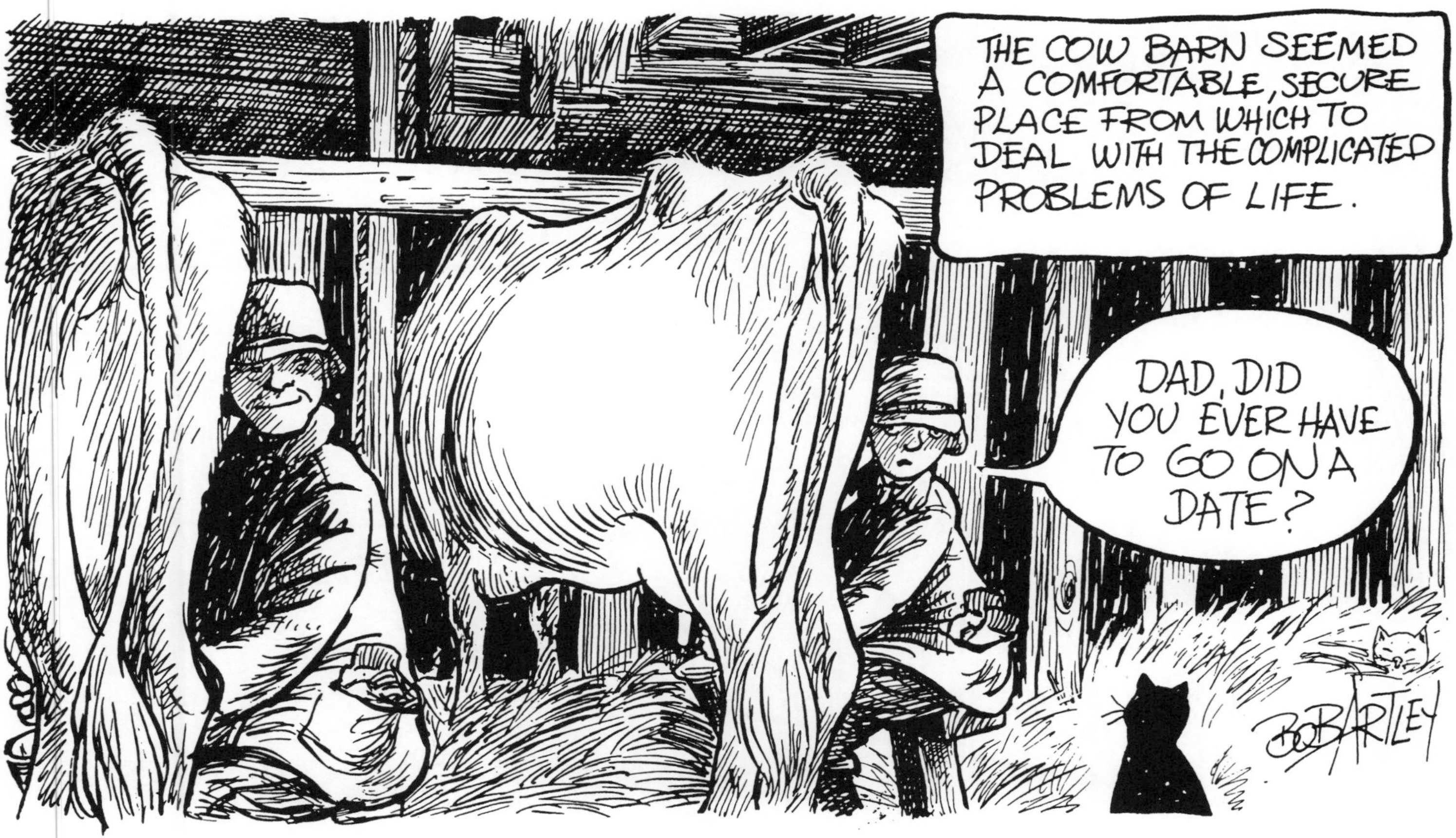
THE COW BARN SEEMED A COMFORTABLE, SECURE PLACE FROM WHICH TO DEAL WITH THE COMPLICATED PROBLEMS OF LIFE.
DAD, DID YOU EVER HAVE TO GO ON A DATE?
BOB ARTLEY

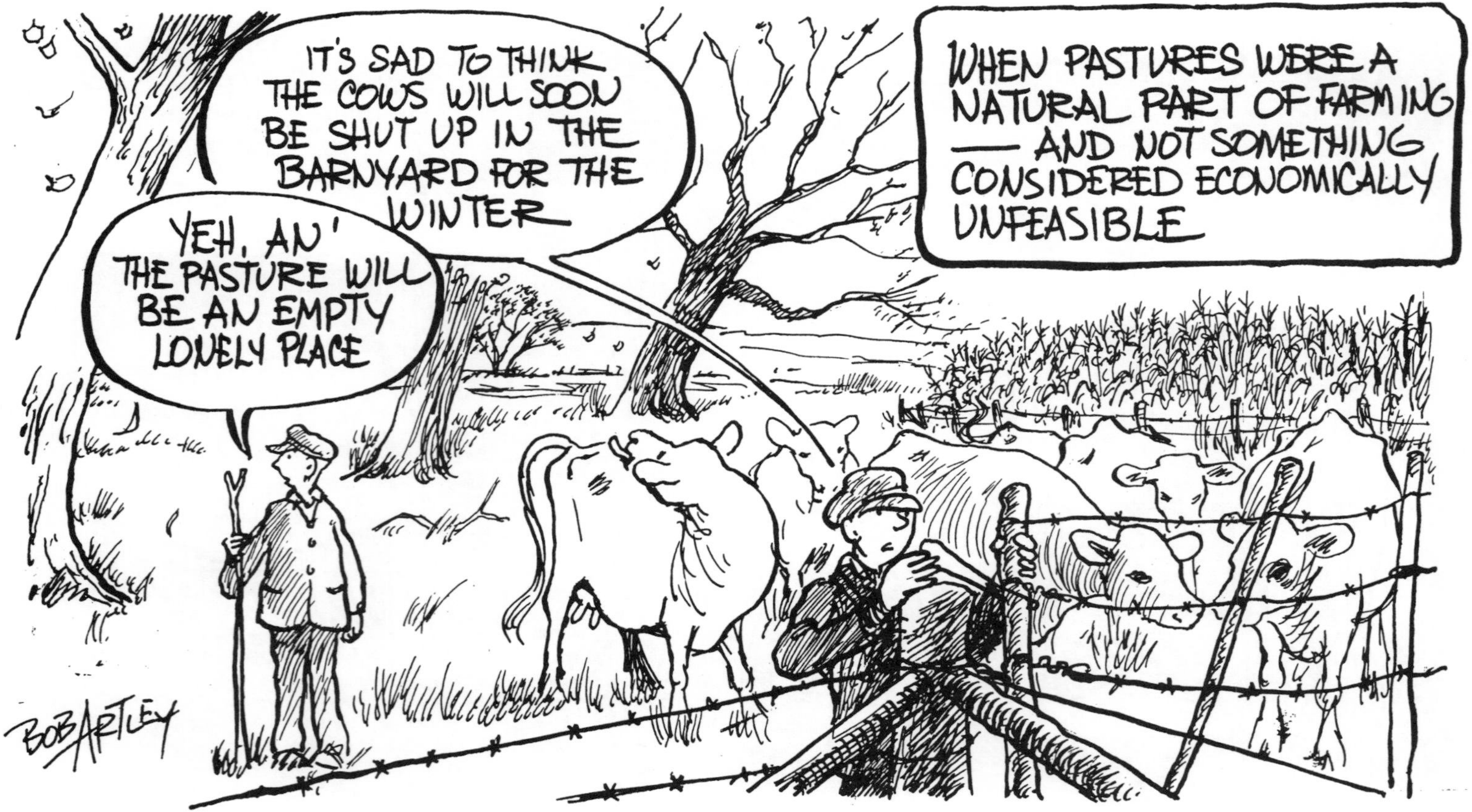
IT'S SAD TO THINK THE COWS WILL SOON BE SHUT UP IN THE BARNYARD FOR THE WINTER
YEH, AN' THE PASTURE WILL BE AN EMPTY LONELY PLACE
WHEN PASTURES WERE A NATURAL PART OF FARMING — AND NOT SOMETHING CONSIDERED ECONOMICALLY UNFEASIBLE
BOB ARTLEY

Cold Hands

During the winter months there was always the problem of keeping our hands and feet from getting frostbite while doing chores around the farmyard.

On our feet we wore one or two pairs of heavy wool socks, leather work shoes, and a pair of four- or five-buckle, flannel-lined overshoes. We would swing and stamp our feet in an effort to keep the blood circulating. But even with all of those efforts, long before we had finished trudging back and forth through the snow and ice of the barnyard, our toes became like balls of ice and we looked longingly to when we could go into the house and soak our bare feet in a pan of tepid water, hoping to avert frostbite and resulting chilblains.

Our hands were covered by at least two pairs of cotton flannel mittens. But even so, after an hour of grasping the icy handles of forks and scoop shovels and the bails of buckets as we dipped them into the ice-fringed water of the stock tank, carrying water to the pigs, chickens and calves, our fingers were tingling or aching with the cold.

Thus it was that we looked forward to our trip into the cow

barn when we could warm our hands on the warm udders and teats of the milk cows.

This fringe benefit of milking by hand must have been anything but pleasant for the poor cows. They would often start slightly and each would turn her head and look at me with a doleful eye, when upon first sitting down to milk I'd slip my cold hands up into the warm pockets formed between the full udder and soft flanks.

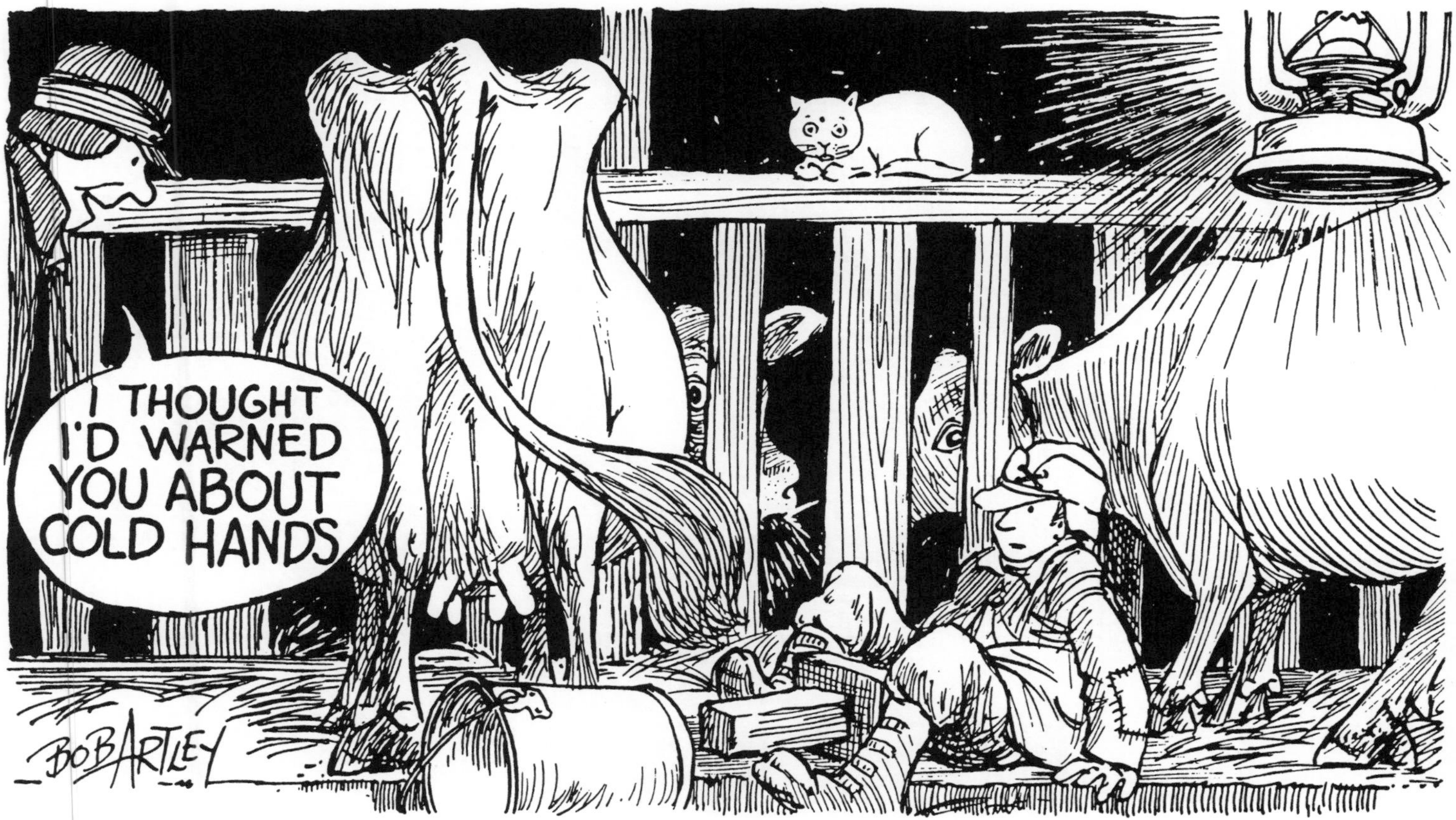
I THOUGHT I'D WARNED YOU ABOUT COLD HANDS
BOB BARTLEY

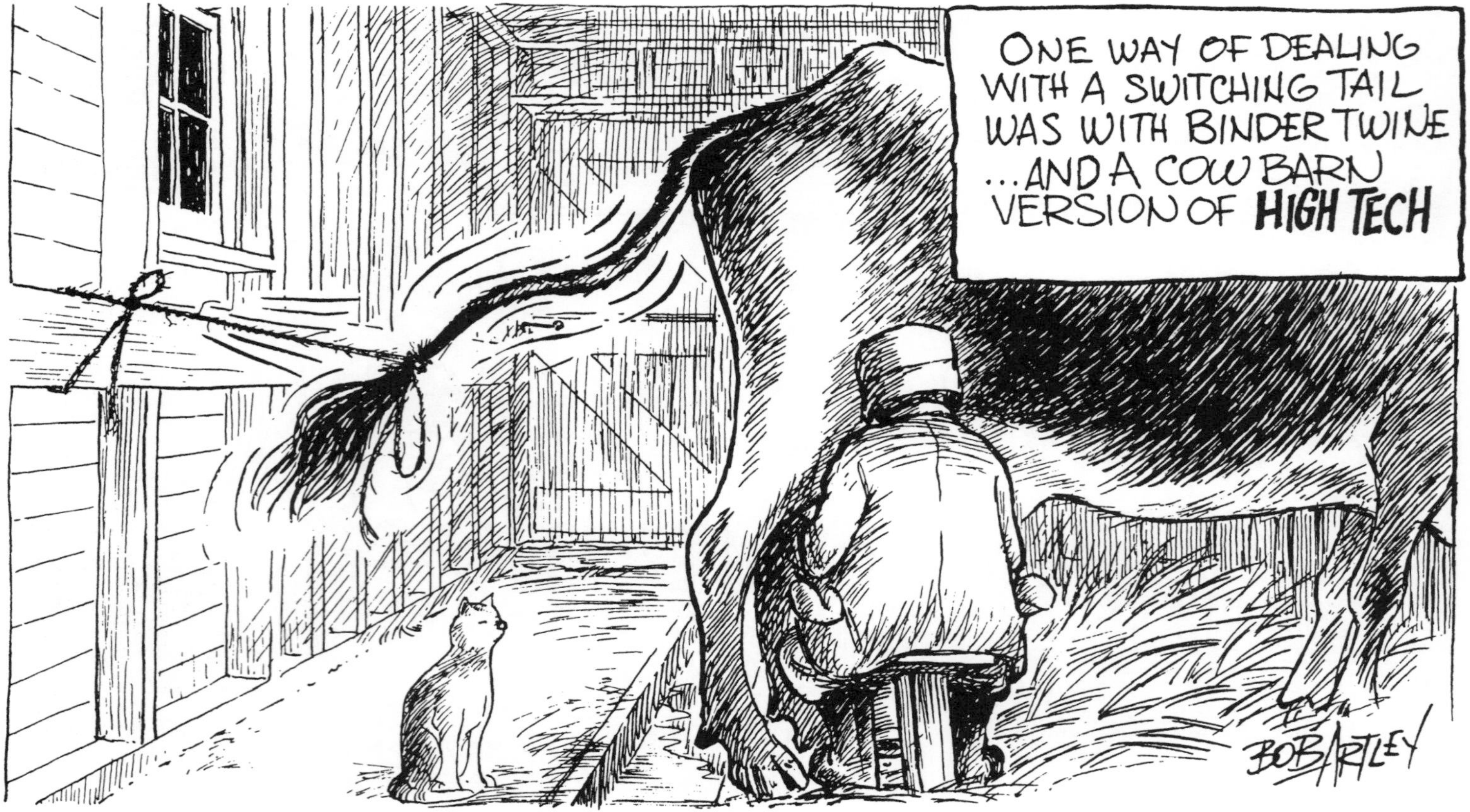
ONE WAY OF DEALING WITH A SWITCHING TAIL WAS WITH BINDER TWINE ...AND A COW BARN VERSION OF HIGH TECH
BOB ARTLEY

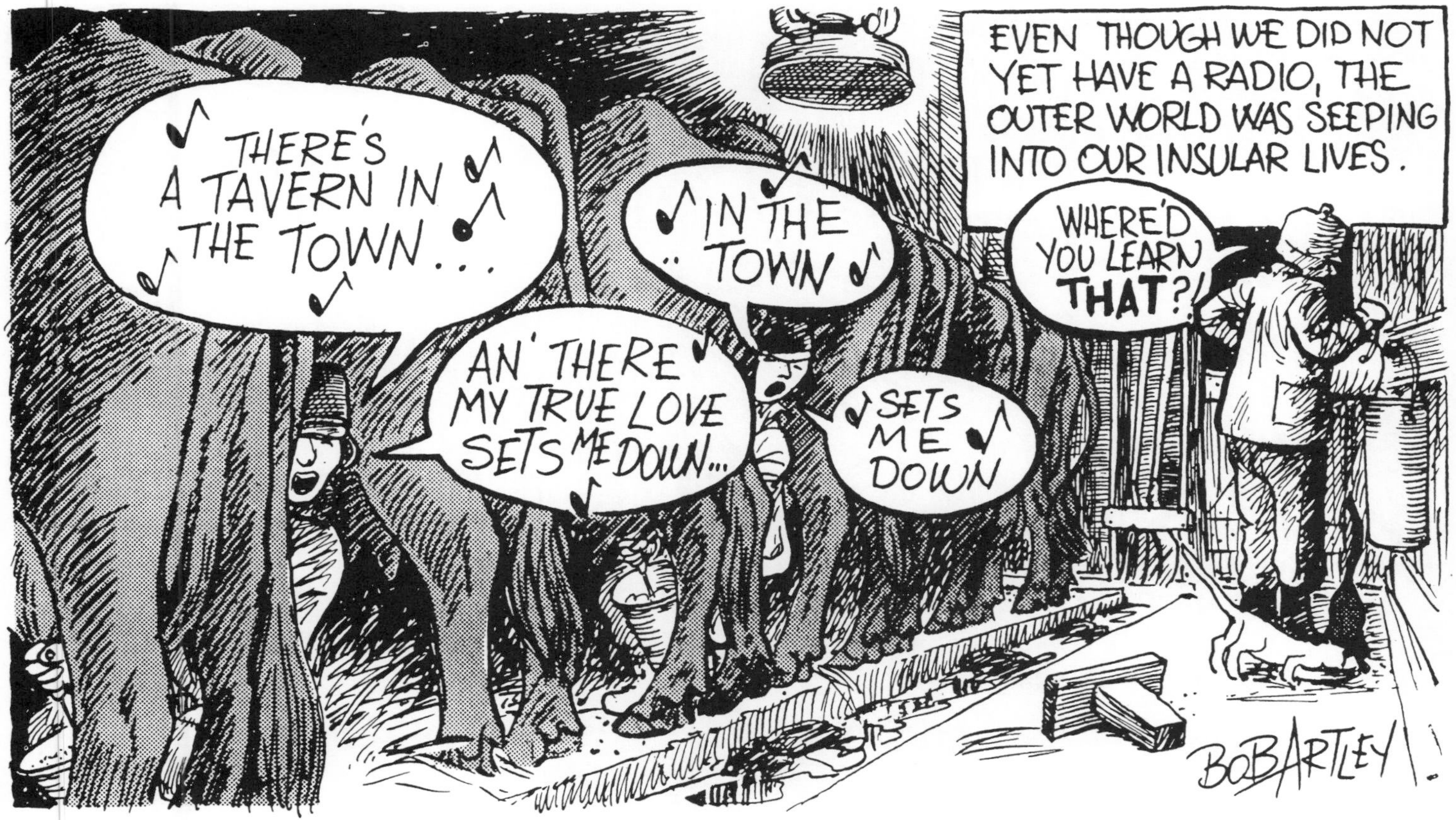
EVEN THOUGH WE DID NOT YET HAVE A RADIO, THE OUTER WORLD WAS SEEPING INTO OUR INSULAR LIVES.
THERE'S A TAVERN IN THE TOWN....
IN THE TOWN
AN' THERE MY TRUE LOVE SETS ME DOWN...
SETS ME DOWN
WHERE'D YOU LEARN THAT?!
BOBARTLEY

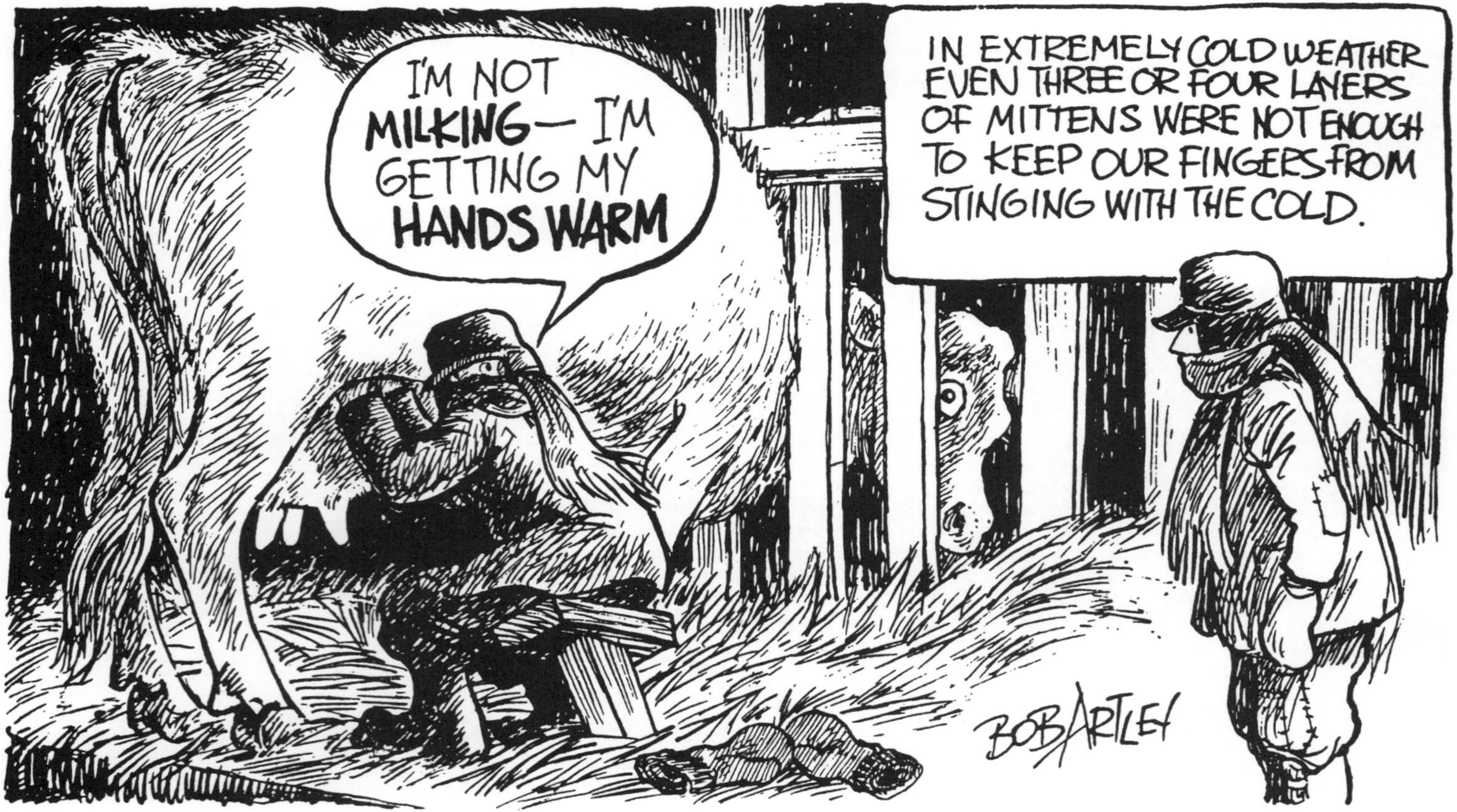
I'M NOT MILKING— I'M GETTING MY HANDS WARM
IN EXTREMELY COLD WEATHER EVEN THREE OR FOUR LAYERS OF MITTENS WERE NOT ENOUGH TO KEEP OUR FINGERS FROM STINGING WITH THE COLD.
BOB ARTLEY

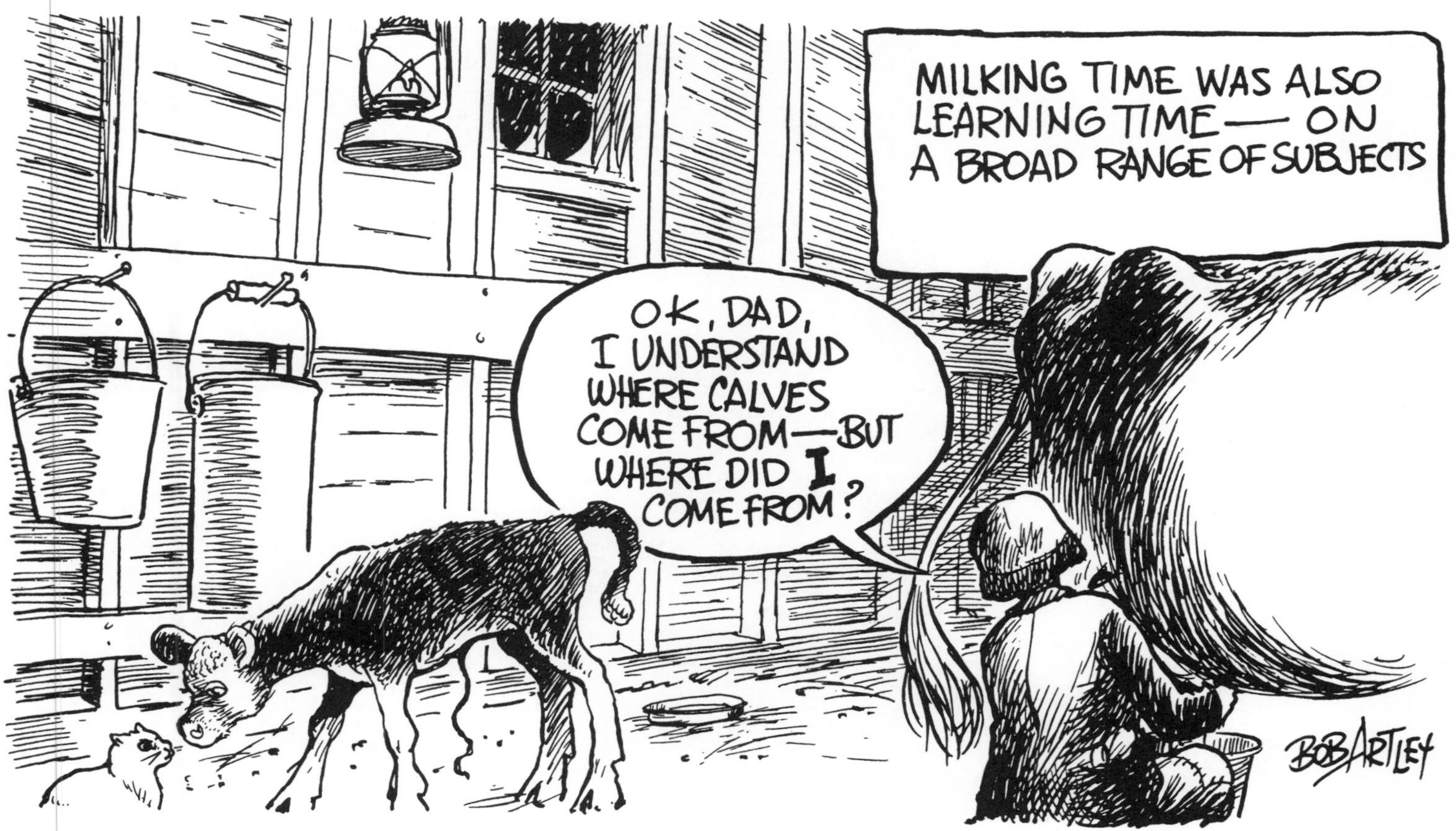
MILKING TIME WAS ALSO LEARNING TIME — ON A BROAD RANGE OF SUBJECTS
OK, DAD, I UNDERSTAND WHERE CALVES COME FROM — BUT WHERE DID I COME FROM?
BOB ARTLEY

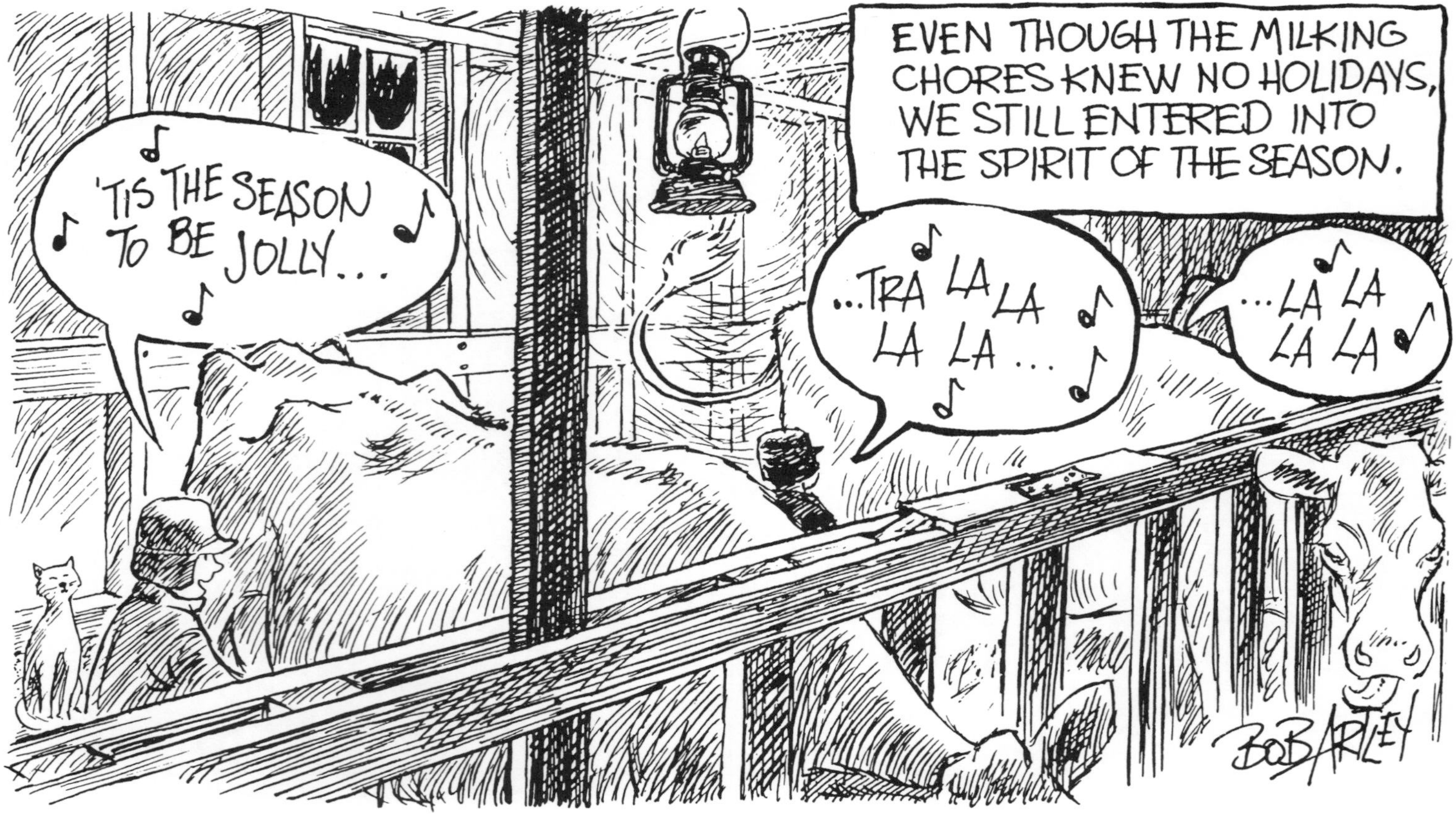
EVEN THOUGH THE MILKING CHORES KNEW NO HOLIDAYS, WE STILL ENTERED INTO THE SPIRIT OF THE SEASON.
'TIS THE SEASON TO BE JOLLY...
...TRA LA LA LA LA...
...LA LA LA LA
BOB ARTLEY

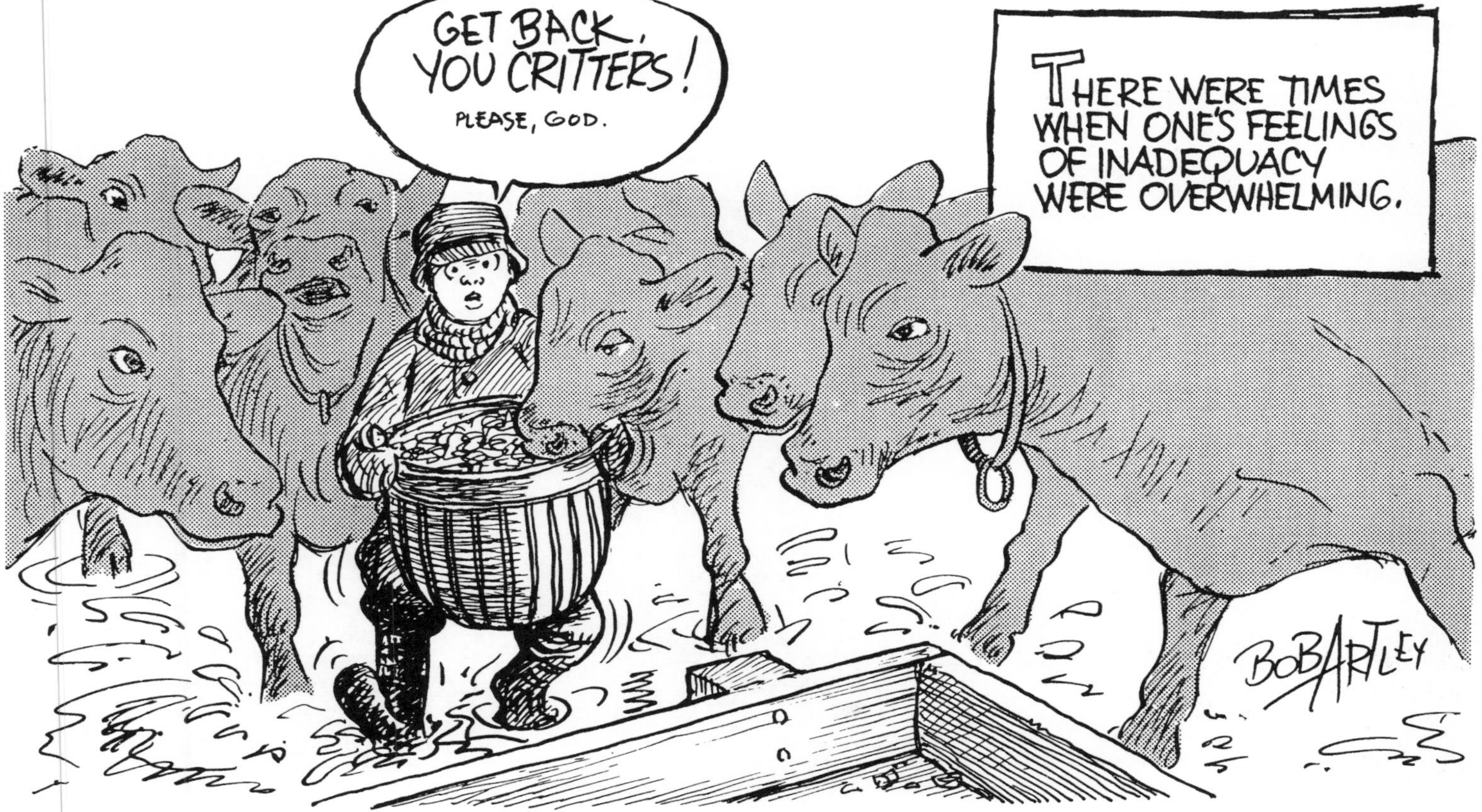
GET BACK, YOU CRITTERS!
PLEASE, GOD.
THERE WERE TIMES WHEN ONE'S FEELINGS OF INADEQUACY WERE OVERWHELMING.
BOB ARTLEY

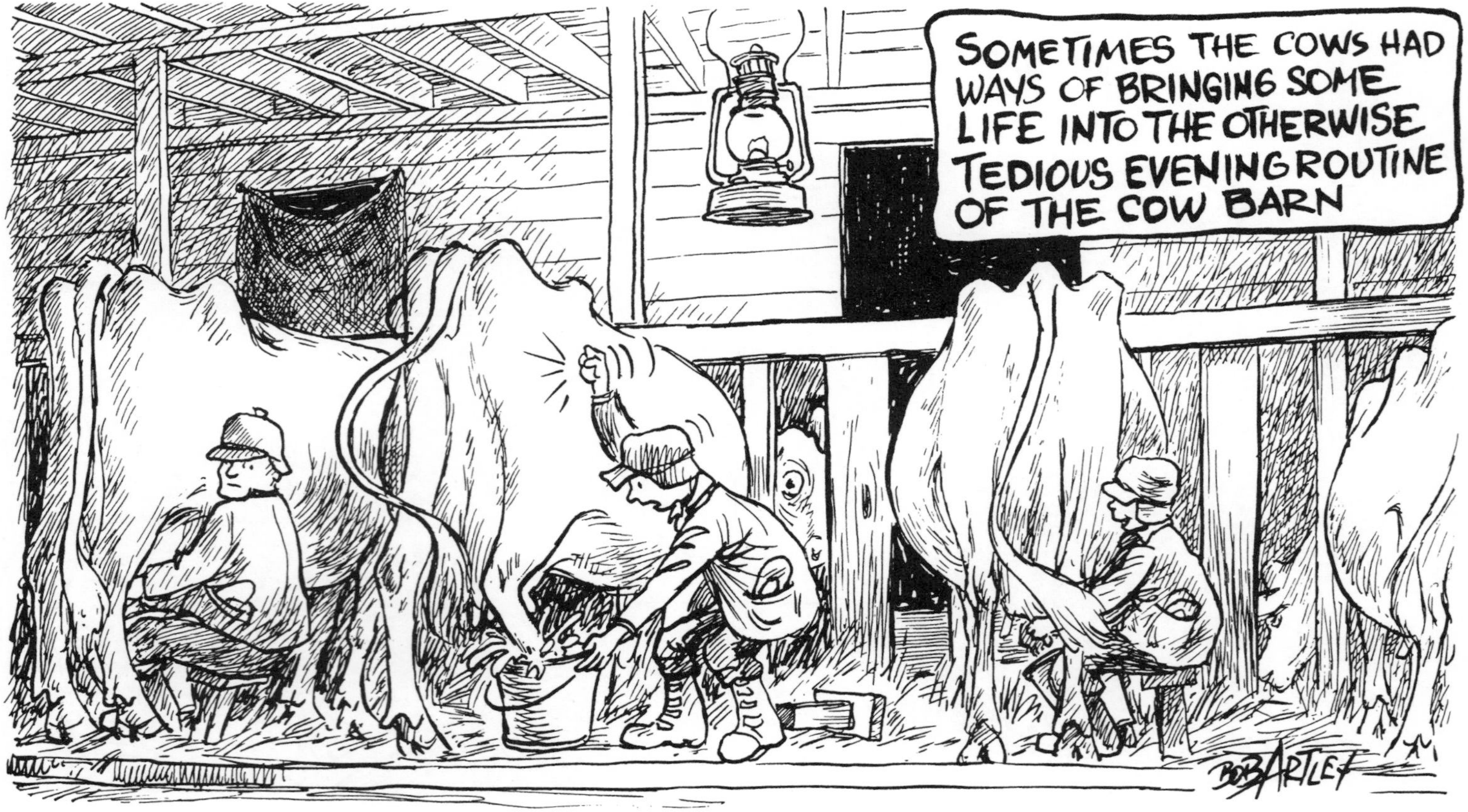
SOMETIMES THE COWS HAD WAYS OF BRINGING SOME LIFE INTO THE OTHERWISE TEDIOUS EVENING ROUTINE OF THE COW BARN
BOB BARTLET

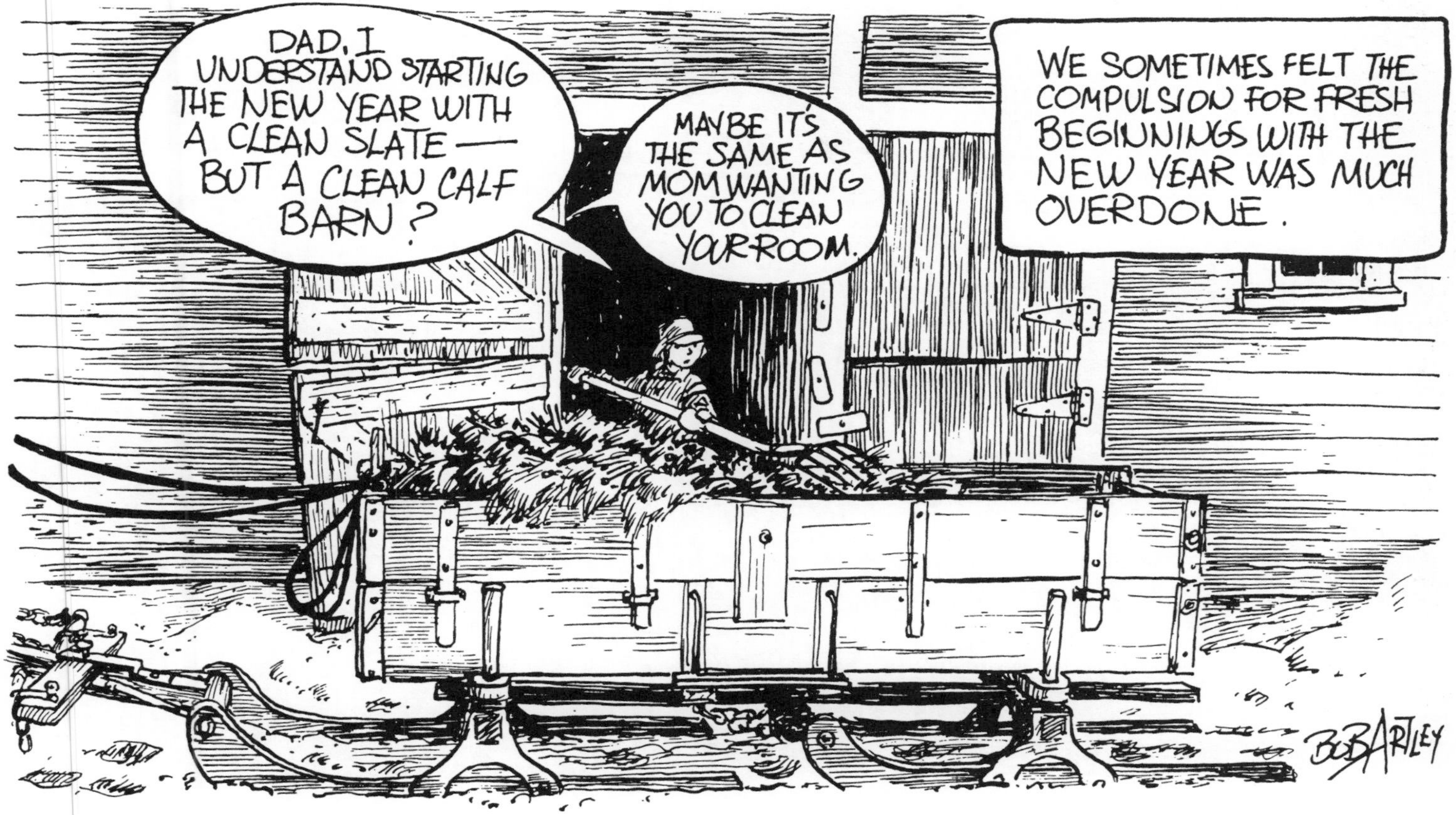
DAD, I UNDERSTAND STARTING THE NEW YEAR WITH A CLEAN SLATE — BUT A CLEAN CALF BARN ?
MAYBE IT'S THE SAME AS MOM WANTING YOU TO CLEAN YOUR ROOM.
WE SOMETIMES FELT THE COMPULSION FOR FRESH BEGINNINGS WITH THE NEW YEAR WAS MUCH OVERDONE.
BOB ARTLEY

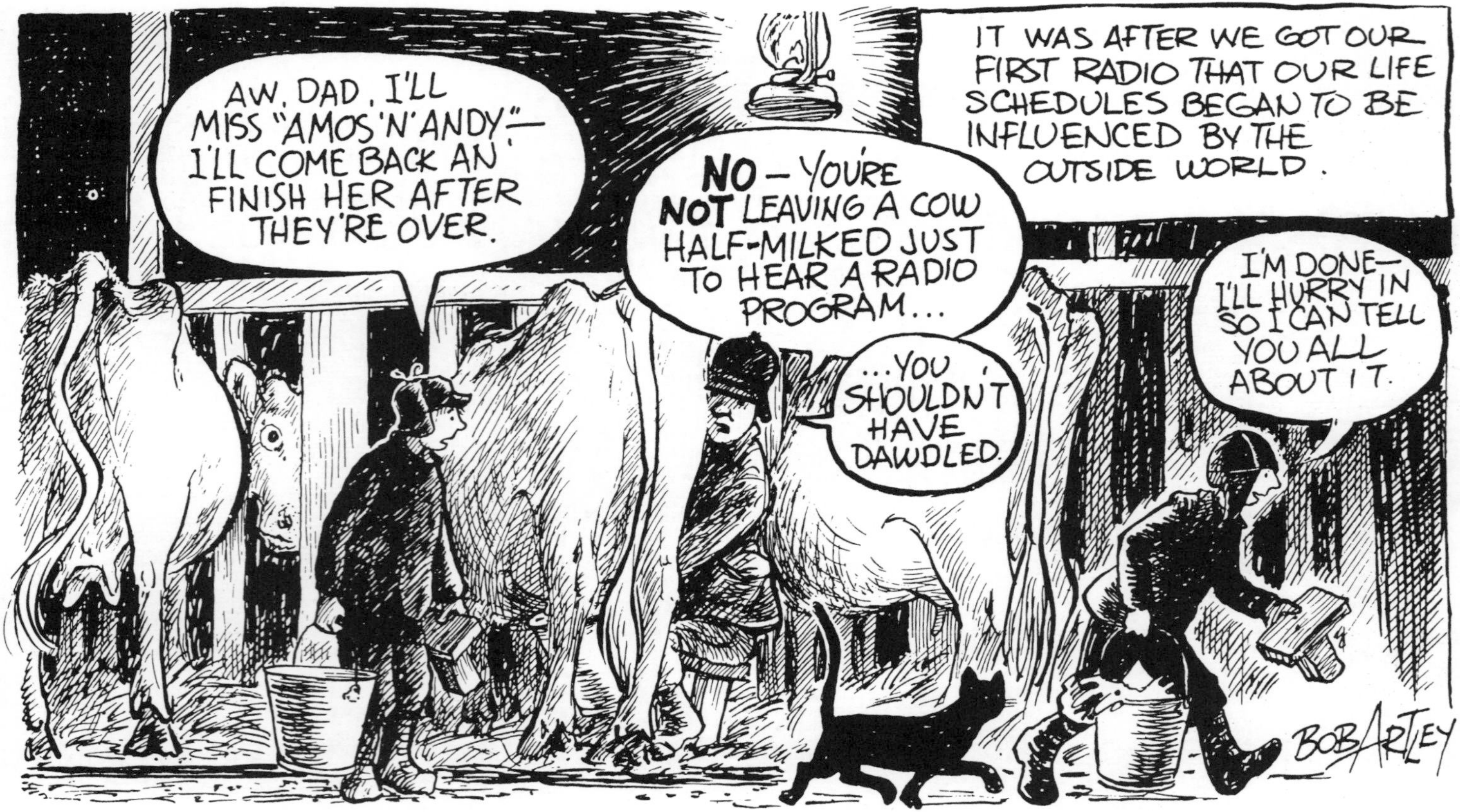
IT WAS AFTER WE GOT OUR FIRST RADIO THAT OUR LIFE SCHEDULES BEGAN TO BE INFLUENCED BY THE OUTSIDE WORLD.
AW, DAD, I'LL MISS "AMOS 'N' ANDY"— I'LL COME BACK AN FINISH HER AFTER THEY'RE OVER.
NO — YOU'RE NOT LEAVING A COW HALF-MILKED JUST TO HEAR A RADIO PROGRAM...
...YOU SHOULDN'T HAVE DAWDLED.
I'M DONE— I'LL HURRY IN SO I CAN TELL YOU ALL ABOUT IT.
BOB ARTLEY

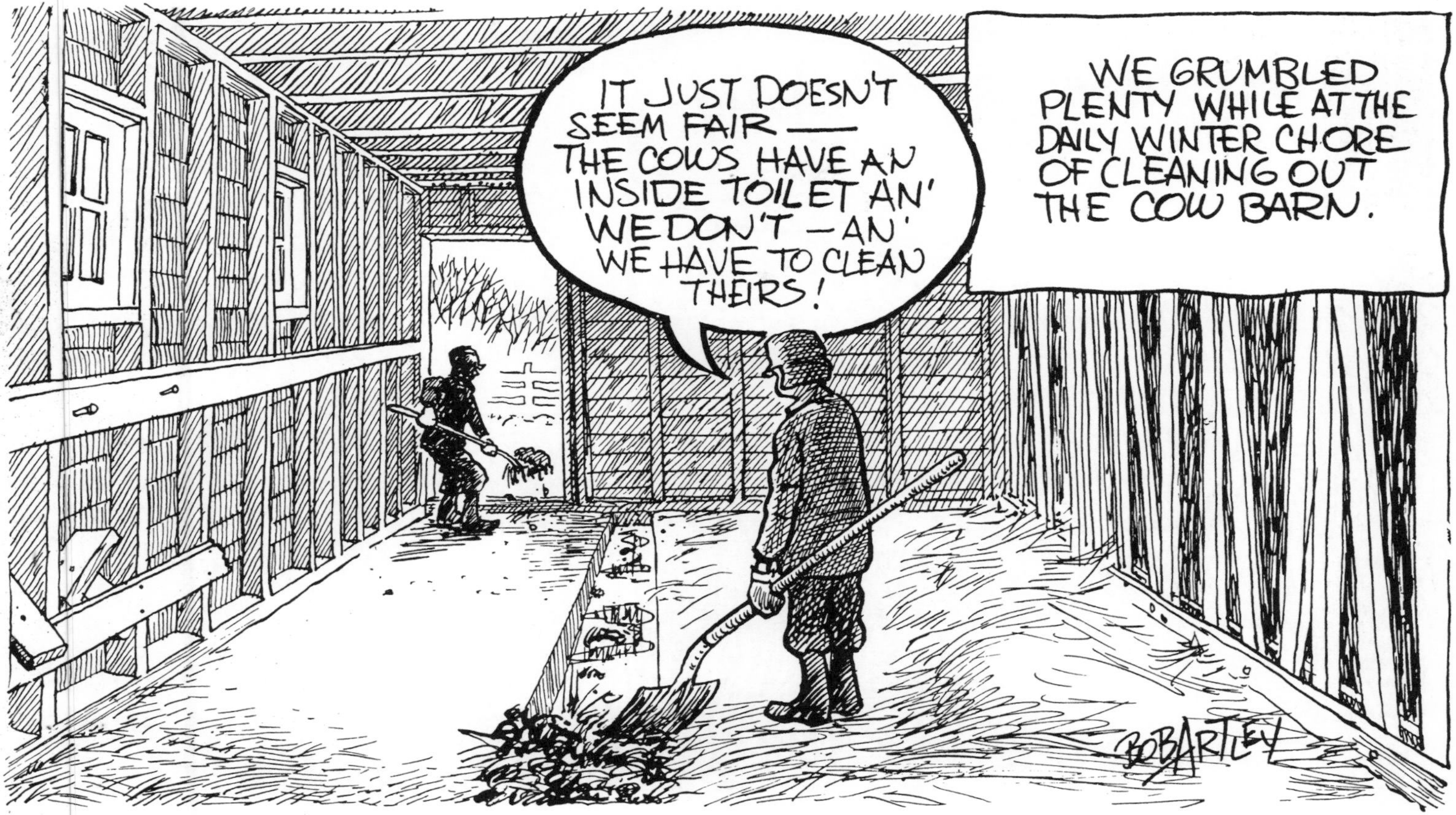
IT JUST DOESN'T SEEM FAIR — THE COWS HAVE AN INSIDE TOILET AN' WE DON'T — AN' WE HAVE TO CLEAN THEIRS!
WE GRUMBLED PLENTY WHILE AT THE DAILY WINTER CHORE OF CLEANING OUT THE COW BARN.
BOB BARTLEY

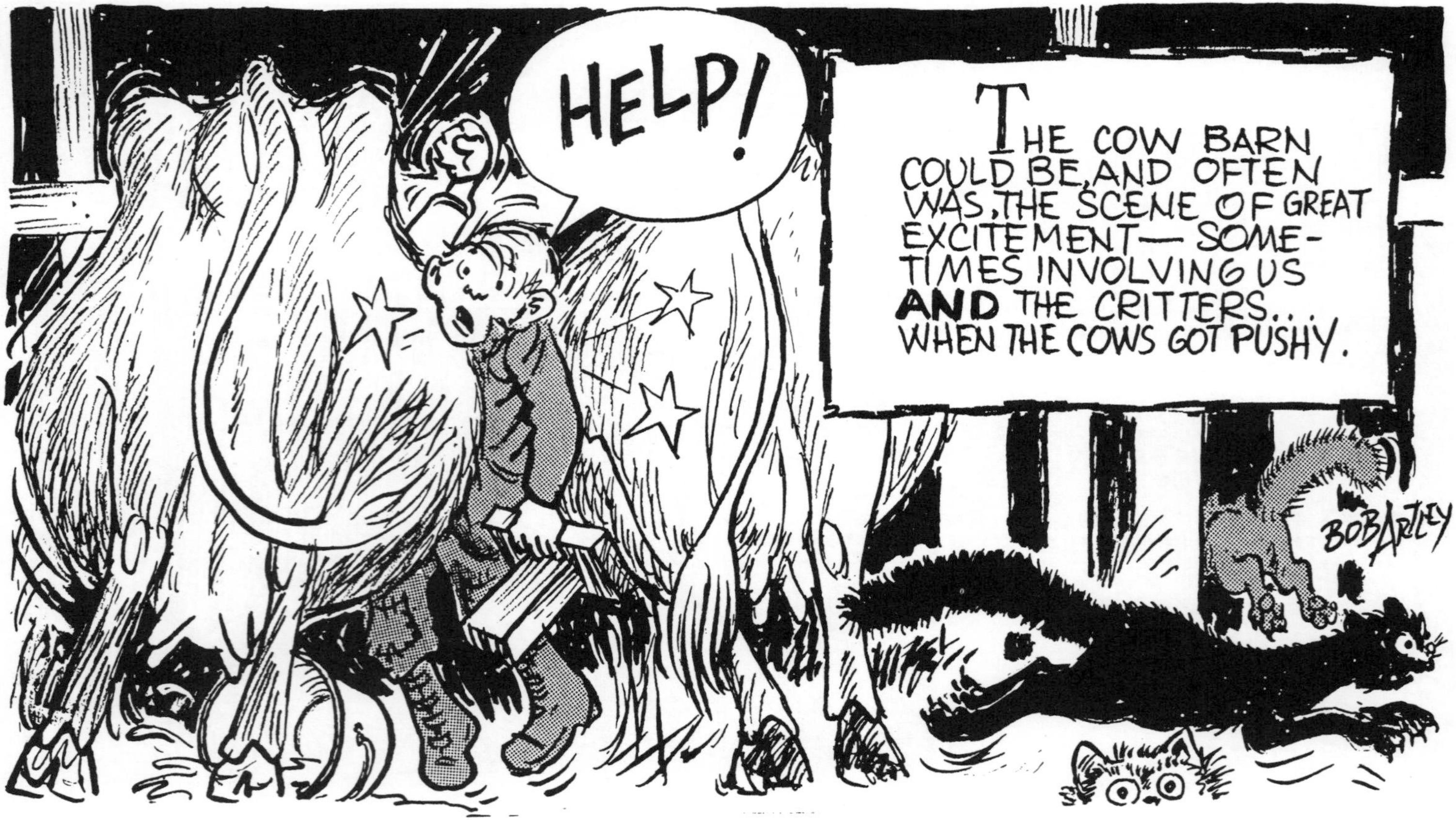
HELP!
THE COW BARN COULD BE, AND OFTEN WAS, THE SCENE OF GREAT EXCITEMENT— SOMETIMES INVOLVING US **AND** THE CRITTERS... WHEN THE COWS GOT PUSHY.
BOB ARTLEY

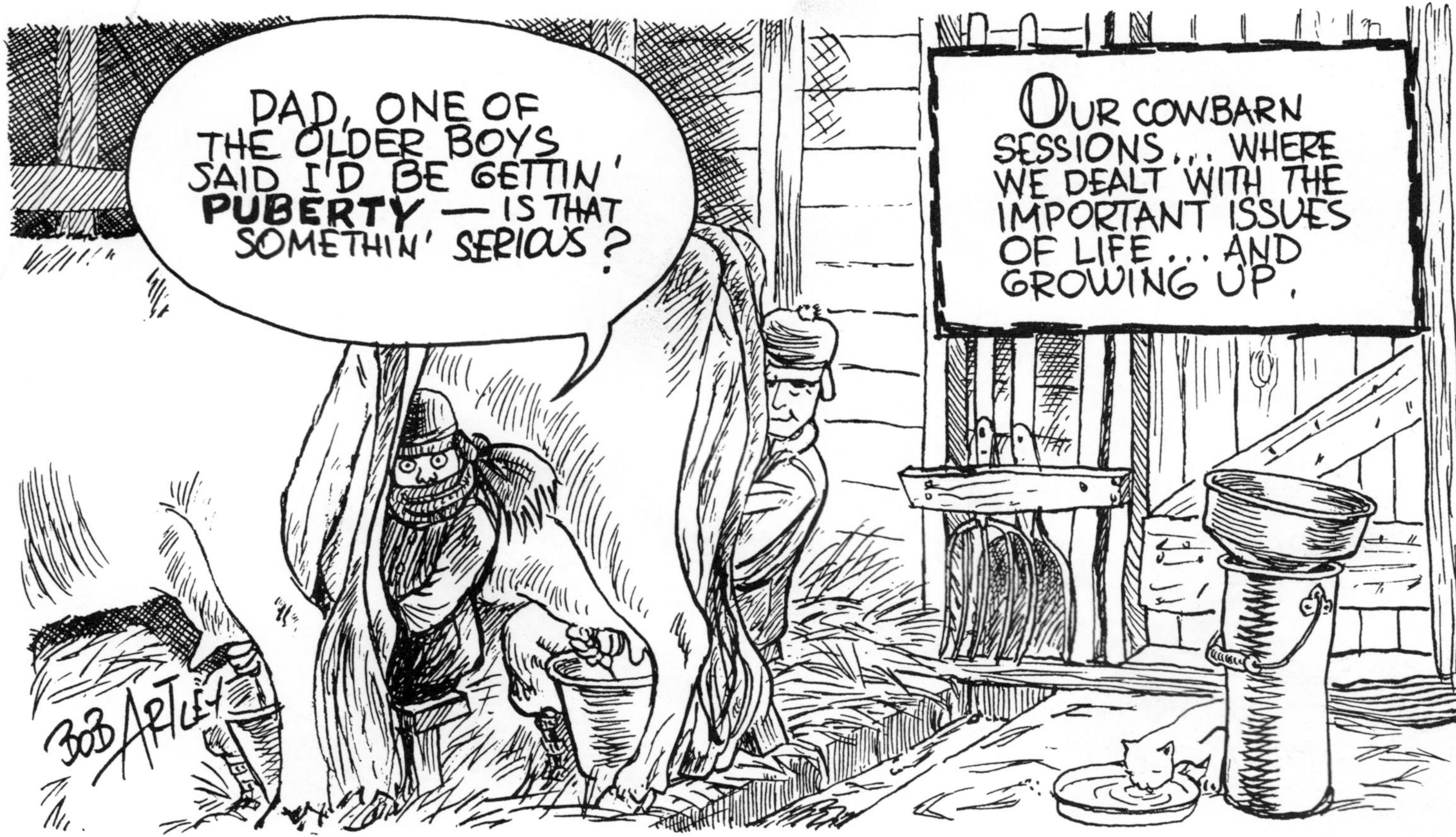
DAD, ONE OF THE OLDER BOYS SAID I'D BE GETTIN' **PUBERTY** — IS THAT SOMETHIN' SERIOUS?
OUR COWBARN SESSIONS... WHERE WE DEALT WITH THE IMPORTANT ISSUES OF LIFE... AND GROWING UP.
BOB ARTLEY

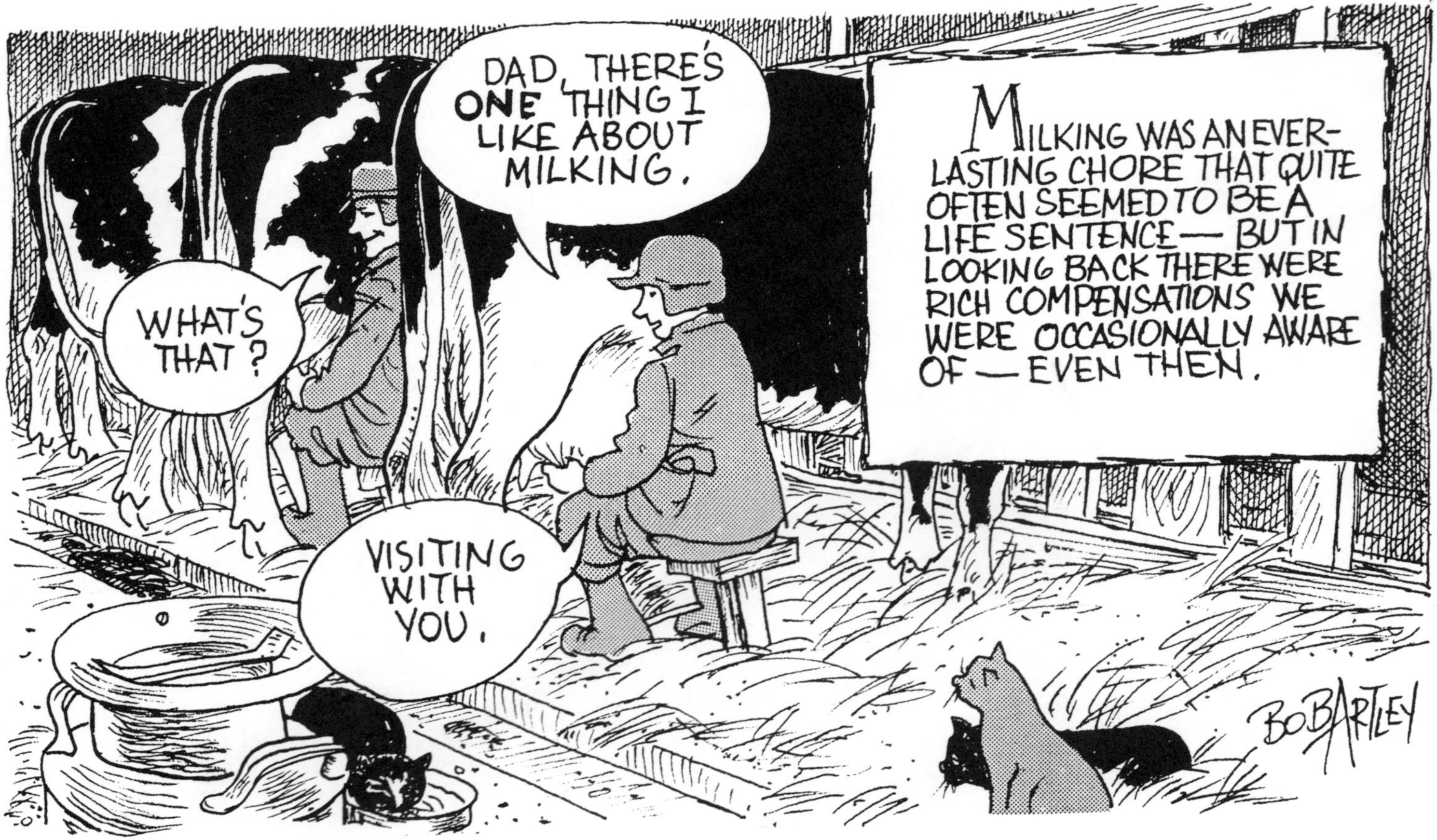
DAD, THERE'S ONE THING I LIKE ABOUT MILKING.
WHAT'S THAT?
VISITING WITH YOU.
MILKING WAS AN EVER-LASTING CHORE THAT QUITE OFTEN SEEMED TO BE A LIFE SENTENCE — BUT IN LOOKING BACK THERE WERE RICH COMPENSATIONS WE WERE OCCASIONALLY AWARE OF — EVEN THEN.
BOB ARTLEY

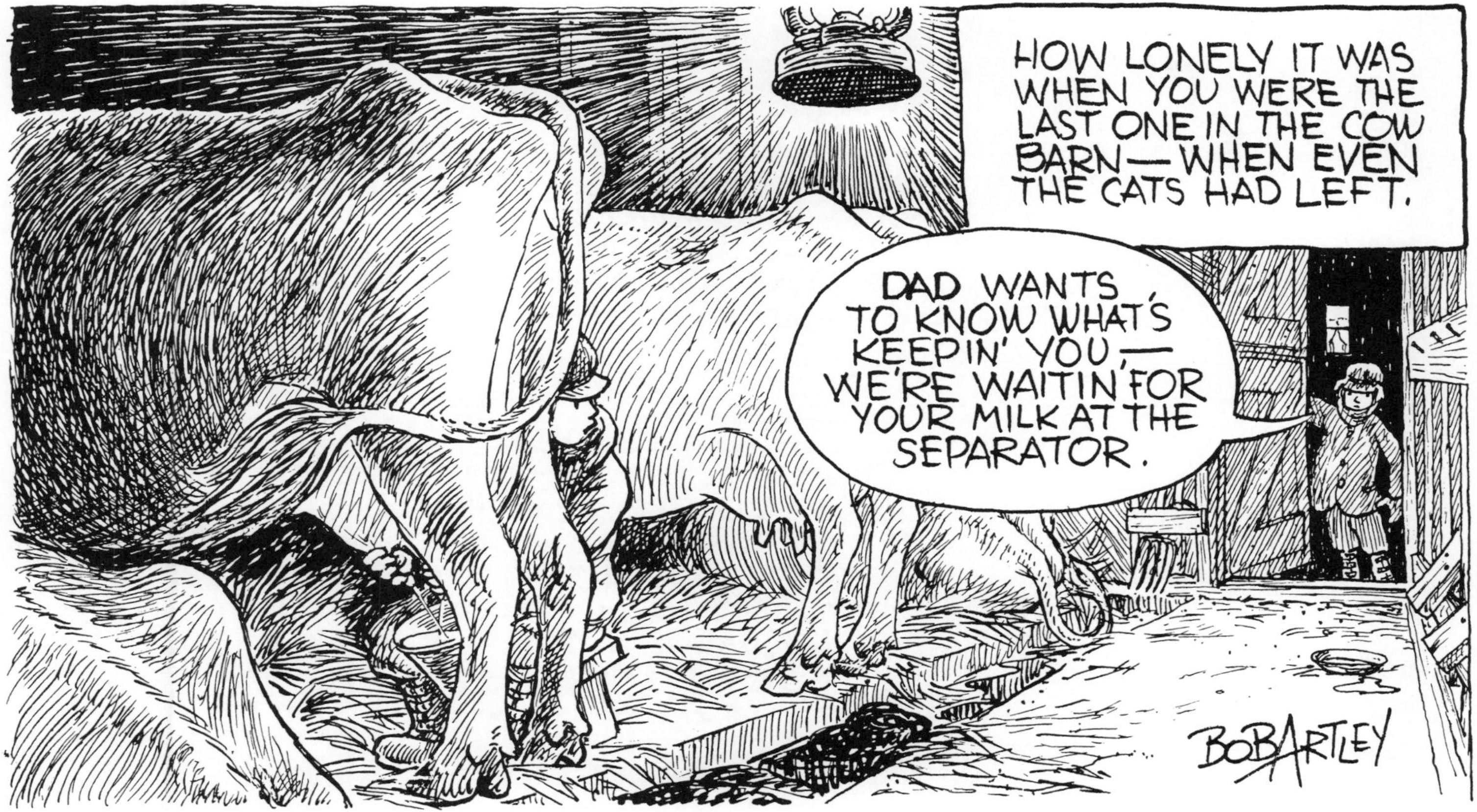
HOW LONELY IT WAS WHEN YOU WERE THE LAST ONE IN THE COW BARN— WHEN EVEN THE CATS HAD LEFT.
DAD WANTS TO KNOW WHAT'S KEEPIN' YOU— WE'RE WAITIN' FOR YOUR MILK AT THE SEPARATOR.
BOB ARTLEY

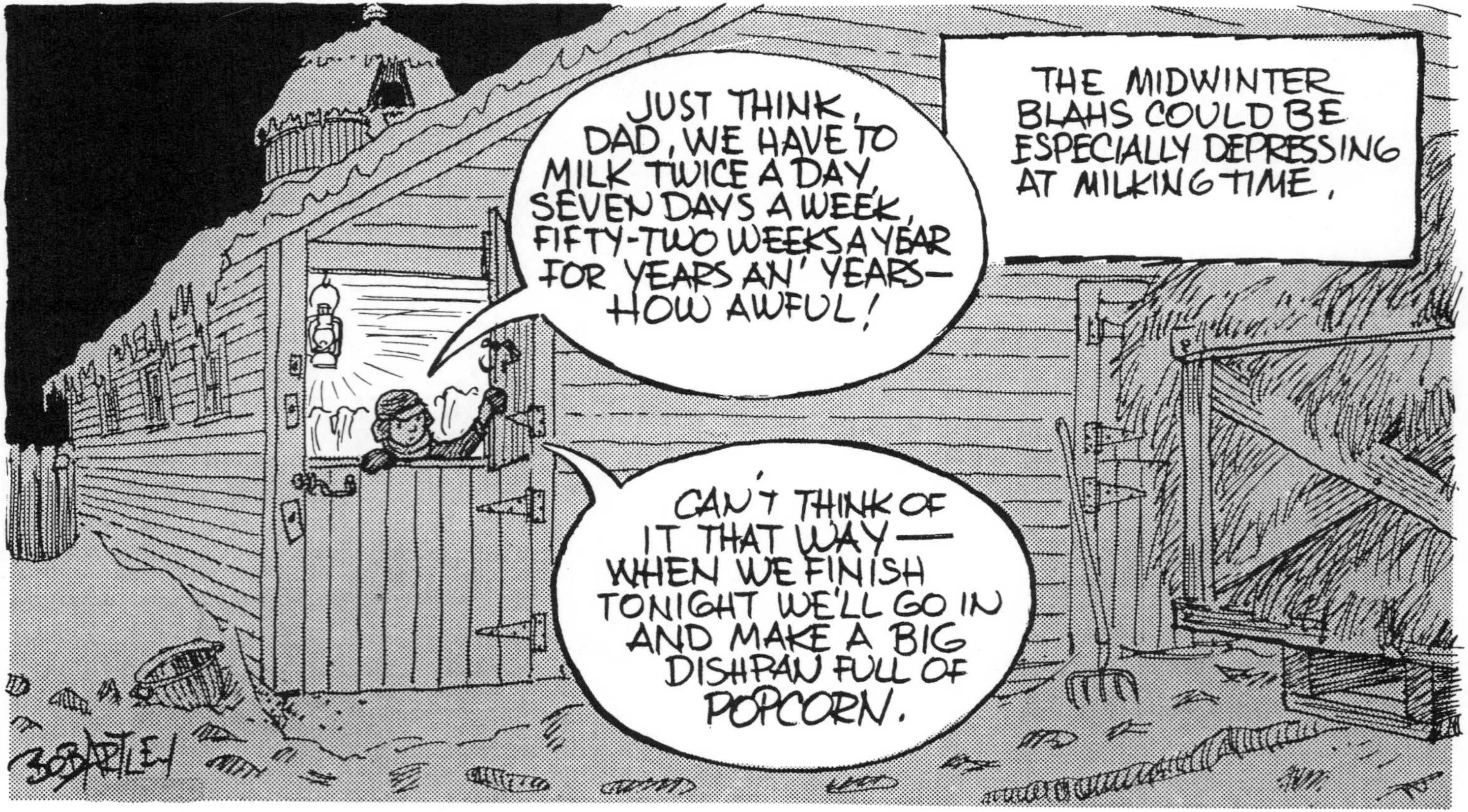
THE MIDWINTER BLAHS COULD BE ESPECIALLY DEPRESSING AT MILKING TIME.
JUST THINK, DAD, WE HAVE TO MILK TWICE A DAY, SEVEN DAYS A WEEK, FIFTY-TWO WEEKS A YEAR FOR YEARS AN' YEARS— HOW AWFUL!
CAN'T THINK OF IT THAT WAY— WHEN WE FINISH TONIGHT WE'LL GO IN AND MAKE A BIG DISHPAN FULL OF POPCORN.
BOB ARTLEY

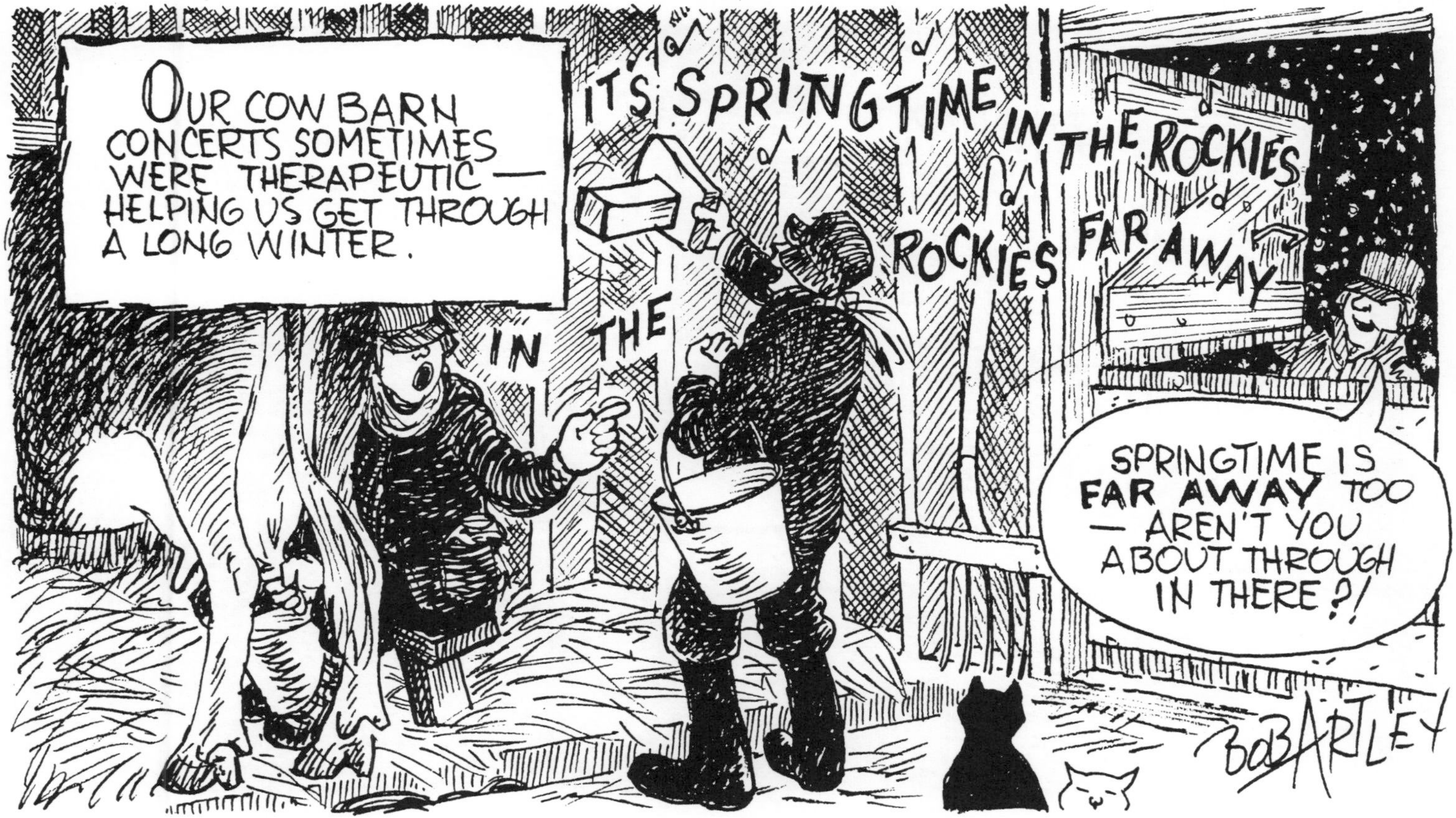
OUR COW BARN CONCERTS SOMETIMES WERE THERAPEUTIC — HELPING US GET THROUGH A LONG WINTER.
IT'S SPRINGTIME IN THE ROCKIES
IN THE ROCKIES FAR AWAY
SPRINGTIME IS **FAR AWAY** TOO — AREN'T YOU ABOUT THROUGH IN THERE?!
BOB ARTLEY

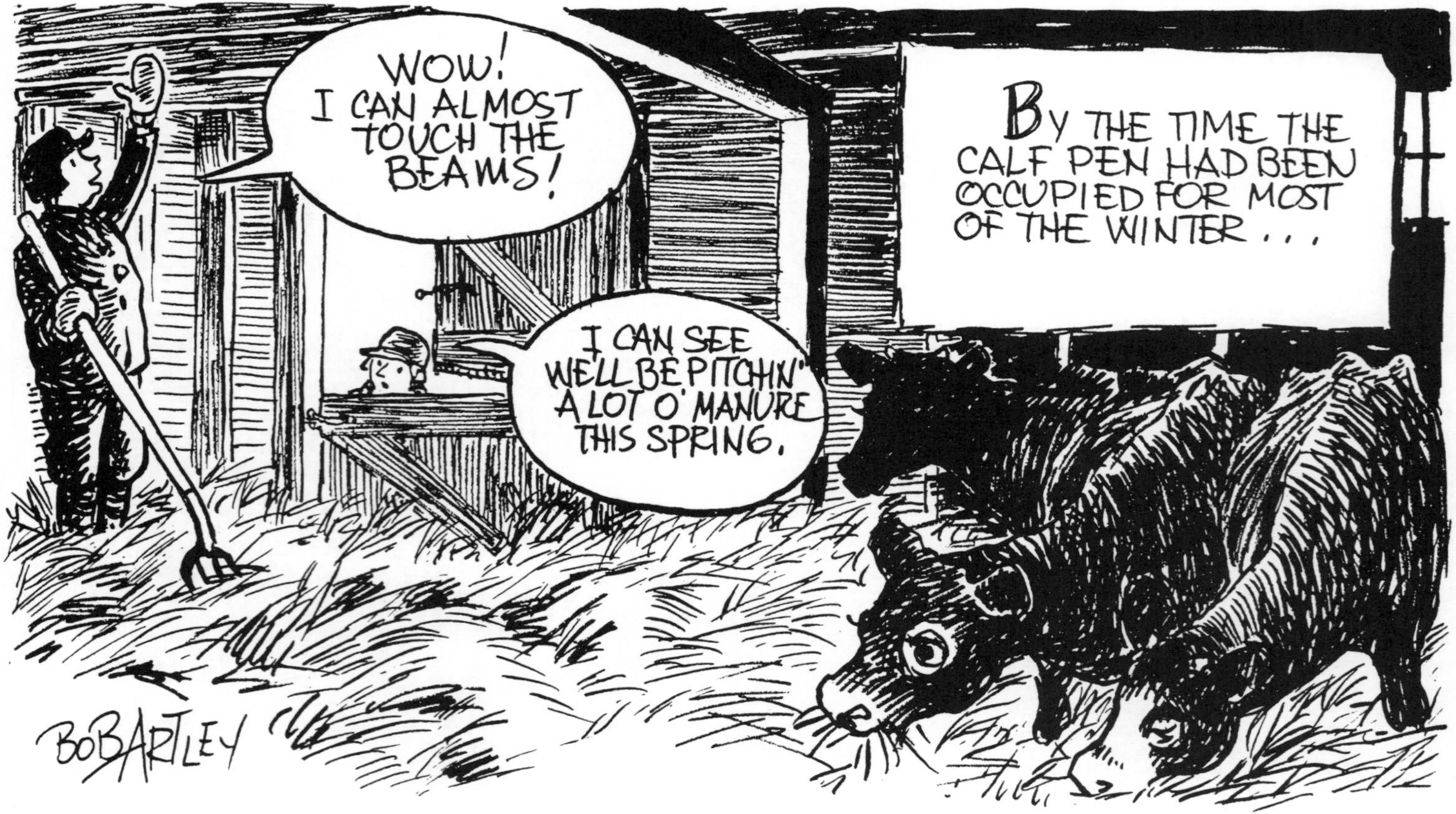
BY THE TIME THE CALF PEN HAD BEEN OCCUPIED FOR MOST OF THE WINTER . . .
WOW! I CAN ALMOST TOUCH THE BEAMS!
I CAN SEE WE'LL BE PITCHIN' A LOT O' MANURE THIS SPRING.
BOB ARTLEY

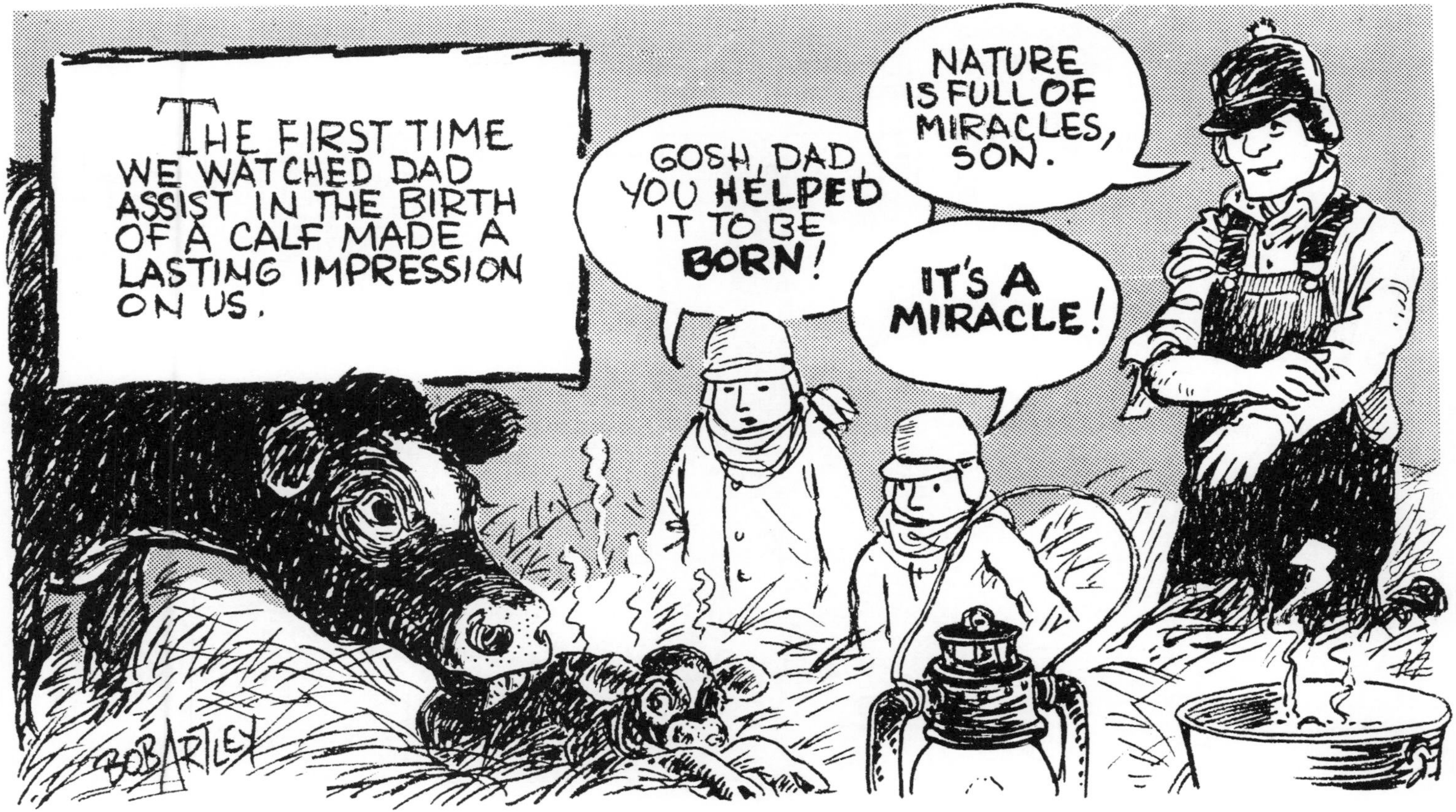
THE FIRST TIME WE WATCHED DAD ASSIST IN THE BIRTH OF A CALF MADE A LASTING IMPRESSION ON US.
GOSH, DAD, YOU **HELPED** IT TO BE **BORN**!
NATURE IS FULL OF MIRACLES, SON.
IT'S A MIRACLE!
BOBARTLEY

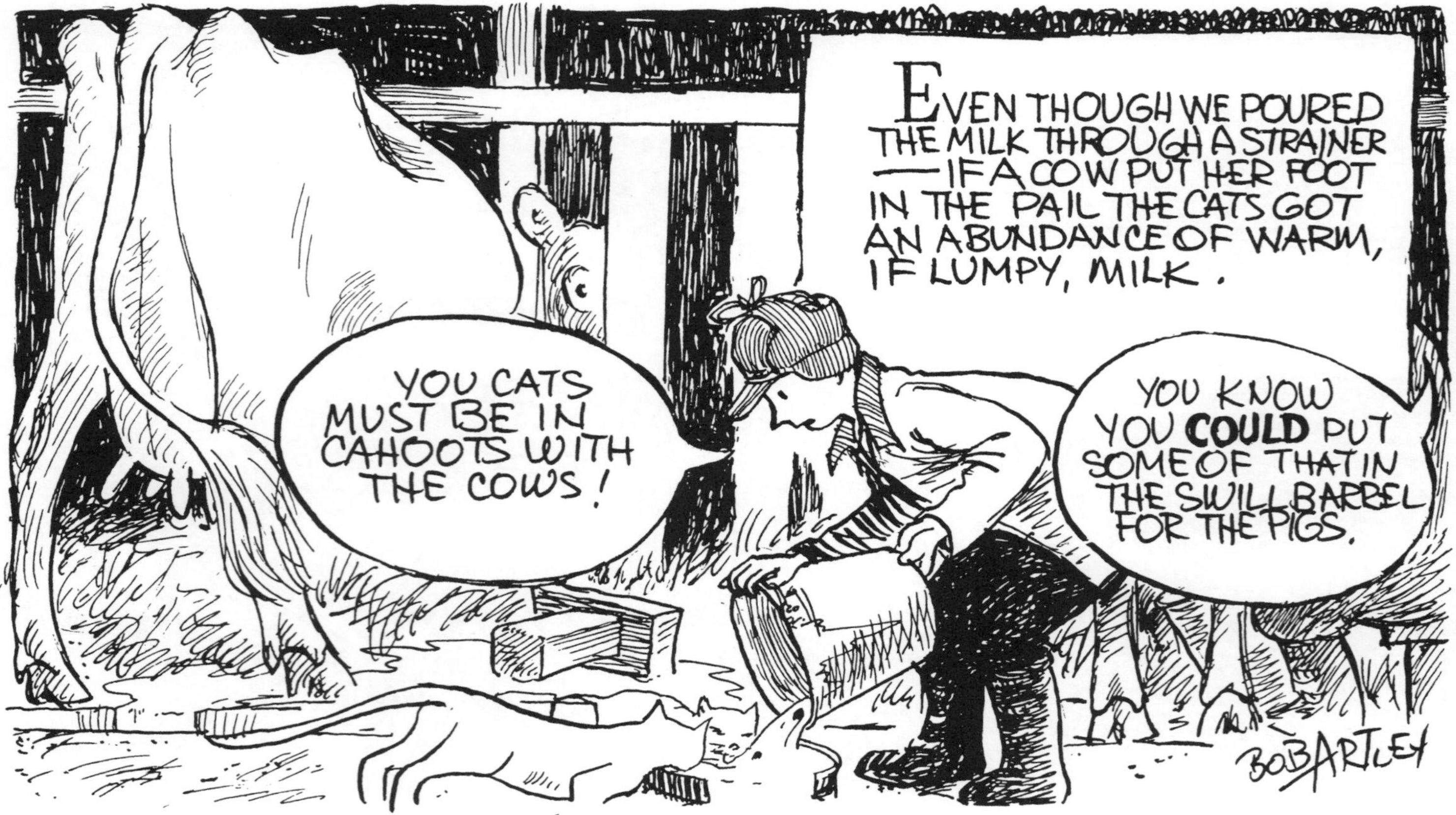
EVEN THOUGH WE POURED THE MILK THROUGH A STRAINER — IF A COW PUT HER FOOT IN THE PAIL THE CATS GOT AN ABUNDANCE OF WARM, IF LUMPY, MILK.
YOU CATS MUST BE IN CAHOOTS WITH THE COWS!
YOU KNOW YOU **COULD** PUT SOME OF THAT IN THE SWILL BARREL FOR THE PIGS.
BOB ARTLEY

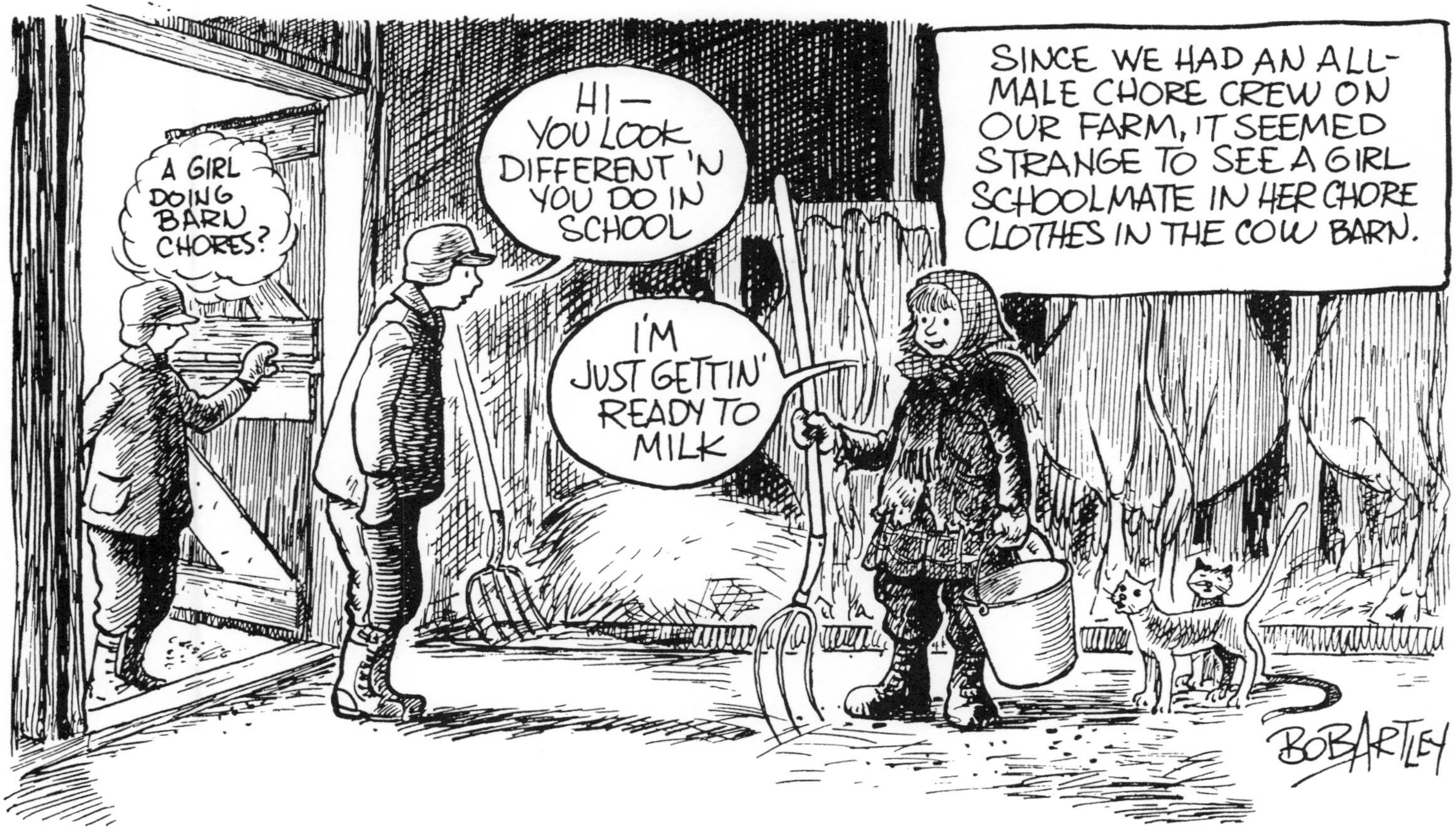
A GIRL DOING BARN CHORES?
HI— YOU LOOK DIFFERENT 'N YOU DO IN SCHOOL
SINCE WE HAD AN ALL-MALE CHORE CREW ON OUR FARM, IT SEEMED STRANGE TO SEE A GIRL SCHOOLMATE IN HER CHORE CLOTHES IN THE COW BARN.
I'M JUST GETTIN' READY TO MILK
BOB ARTLEY